Nova Scotia drink-o-pedia

by Graham Pilsworth

Nimbus Publishing Limited
PO Box 9166, Halifax, NS B3K 5M8
(902) 455-4286 www.nimbus.ca

Printed and bound in Canada

All archival images courtesy Nova Scotia Archives and Records Management.
All contemporary photos and illustrations courtesy of the author.

Design: Aaron Harpell

Library and Archives Canada Cataloguing in Publication

Pilsworth, Graham, 1944-
Nova Scotia drink-o-pedia / Graham Pilsworth.
Includes index.
Subtitle: Including rum, beer, wine, whisky, moonshine, tea, coffee, soda, and water. Legends and lore, notorious characters, factoids, trivia, and more!
ISBN 978-1-55109-652-0

1. Drinking of alcoholic beverages—Nova Scotia—History. 2. Alcoholic beverage industry—Nova Scotia—History. 3. Beverage industry—Nova Scotia—History. 4. Drinking customs—Nova Scotia—History. I. Title.

HV5309.N6P54 2008 394.1'309716 C2008-902742-6

Canada
The Canada Council for the Arts | Le Conseil des Arts du Canada
NOVA SCOTIA
Tourism, Culture and Heritage

We acknowledge the financial support of the Government of Canada through the Book Publishing Industry Development Program (BPIDP) and the Canada Council, and of the Province of Nova Scotia through the Department of Tourism, Culture and Heritage for our publishing activities.

APERITIF

Eons ago, Socrates advised: Know thyself. From that challenge forward, societies, countries, and hamlets have spent inordinate amounts of time and sweat equity defining and redefining themselves. Who are we? What are we? What image of ourselves do we present to outsiders and to the greater world at large? Someone once claimed that nothing is more revealing of a province or nation than its art and literature. Few would quibble with that. However, that said, Nova Scotia has been, on the whole, well-served in the defining process by its beverages. Drink, from Nova Scotia's earliest records and accounts, stood in as the rules of the wild and wilderness, the passage-lines of route-maps, and the pattern-cutters of community and class structure mores.

Beverage's story arc embraces the hip and the less than noble: the truths and lies, myths and realities, dreams, nightmares, high times and sober—more than enough jaw-droppers to give one a case of the staggers. Or at least the confirmation that, in a whole lot of instances in this province's past, rationality had points of no return, rife with wily scoundrels at its margins. Characters such as Joshua Mauger (1725–1788), a sketchy Type-A personality enterpriser if there ever was one, moving and shaking successfully in the provincial spirits world.

Beverages altered the lives of Nova Scotians in ways wondrously eclectic, rambunctious, nervy, and daring. Thanks to beverage, if Nova Scotia were a ceilidh in full roister from 1714 on, drink would be the life of the party.

So sit back. Pour yourself a soothing beverage. Enjoy this fascinating and entertaining selection of Nova Scotia's beverage lore, collected and presented in historical vignettes, peopled with outsized characters, full of true-life thrills and chills, pithy songs, sayings, fact-lists, factoids, and nifty visuals.

TABLE OF CONTENTS

RUM

THE RAMBUNCTIOUS REIGN OF KING RUM

Of the many beverages sipped or quaffed in Nova Scotia over its many decades, one qualifies as essential to the province's story. That's rum: stimulant and province-shaper. Rum has been more than merely "a warming tot on a frosty morn." Without rum like a watermark in the pages of our history, Nova Scotia's narrative would have been, to be blunt, a snore. Rum has framed Nova Scotian values, inspired songs, warmed sailors and landlubbers alike forced to brace inclement weather, enlivened recipes, spawned commerce on both sides of the law, and given lifeblood to a bevy of colourful heroes and villains. Indeed, rum has been both mythical and metaphysical in its impact. Try naming another beverage with the cheek for claiming anything close to that. For historians, social scientists, and those of us who enjoy rip-roaring, gutsy, true-life tales, we must give a tip of the hat to rum and say, "We like what you've done to the place."

Today rum is somewhat diminished as a major player in the provincial drinks world, but it's hardly a relic of a bygone era. Nova Scotians to this day continue to keep rum in the top three of popular distillates—the other two being whisky and vodka. The story of rum in the province begins with rum's genesis and the part its creation played in the development of a plucky Nova Scotia–West Indies connection.

RUM-RELATED GLOSSARY

- tot: a small alcoholic beverage serving
- tar: a sailor

TRAVELOGUE OF A PEREGRINATING PLANT

Why the Caribbean dominance in rum production? Look no further than the vast West Indies sugar cane plantations. To make rum, you need cane. How lucky, then, to have such a valuable indigenous plant of your own so close at hand for rum purposes. Except sugar cane wasn't originally native to the West Indies. The fact is, cane cuttings that established the plant in the West crossed the Atlantic with Christopher Columbus in 1493—from the Canary Islands to Hispaniola, now better known as Haiti, and the Dominican Republic. Sugar cane was native to Indonesia, where it served in the early fifteenth century as a trading staple for Chinese, Arab, and Indian traders plying commerce routes between China, Southeast Asia, and India. When trading expanded into North Africa and the Middle East, with it went cane. During the Crusades, Europeans, in particular the Spaniards and the Portuguese, picked up sugar cane. Their expansive business enterprises help explain how cane made it to the Azores, and ultimately to the New World.

WHAT RUM IS AND HOW IT GOT TO BE THAT WAY

Imagine it's the sixteenth century. West Indies sugar cane plantations are cropped by slaves. During the sugar manufacturing process, these slaves catch sight of yeast spores alighting upon pools of uncrystallized cane juice and molasses (the sweet sticky residue remaining after sugar cane juice is boiled and the crystallized sugar extracted), waste by-products of the sugar mill that were tossed aside. The slaves soon make a cool discovery: Much to their delight, natural fermentation produces a potent beer. And when distilled and liquefied, the liquid becomes what we know as rum. As noted in a 1651 Barbados document:

> The chief fuddling [intoxicant] they [plantation slaves] make is Rumbullion [meaning an uproar or huge tumult], alias Kill-Devil [local cure-all for every ill]. This is a hot, hellish and terrible liquor.

As events transpired, these would be ideal qualities for a beverage historically linked to the British Navy, an institution whose traditions inspired the motto-esque quip "Rum, Sodomy, and the Lash."

Jamaica, 1655. Population 4,205, of whom 3,653 are white Spanish settlers, the rest blacks. The island is captured from the Spaniards by the British fleet. Terrified settlers beat a retreat to Cuba. With rum now easily available, the British Navy's daily French brandy gives way to rum rations. With gusto, the fleet's rank and file take to downing a 160-proof rum tot twice a day, either straight or (mercifully for more sensitive gullet linings) cut with lemon juice.

RUM: GOOD FOR WHAT AILS YE

- like sugar, rum's original raison d'etre is a "medicinal-cum-ceremonial luxury potion"
- rum is regarded by sailors as a way to prevent seasickness
- sniffles? An extract of cherries soaked in rum staves off a cold (as does a hot rum toddy)
- for counteracting the effects of rheumatism and to aid alcoholism aversion therapy, try extract of eels immersed in a gallon of rum

OLD GROG AND THE NAVAL TOT TRADITION

The father of grog, Vice-Admiral Edward Vernon (1684–1757), a noted and enlightened advocate of better shipboard conditions and kinder treatment of sailors, and a fierce derider of press-gang naval recruitment, changed the tot by cutting the spirit with water. "Old Grog"—a nickname derived from a waterproof cloak made of grogam (a blend of silk, mohair, and wool stiffened with gum) Vernon wore in rotten weather—initiated grog mixing on deck overseen by the lieutenant of the watch: "One quart of water to one half-pint of rum." It was Vernon's fervent hope that his crew's unsteadiness at sea would mainly be the result of wave action and not rum issue.

➪ The makeup of the tars' grog mixture was based on the direction they were heading.

- due north: pure rum
- due west: water alone
- west northwest: one-third rum, two-thirds water
- northwest: half and half

➪ The Royal Navy's fishy-named daily rum ration was called the "gill," equal in potency to four double whiskies.

- In 1851, the Admiralty decreased the ration to a half-gill.
- The Canadian Army issued half-gills of rum three times per week during the South African (Boer) War and on an ad hoc basis during World War I.
- In the 1740s, the British Navy grog issue of one gill (five ounces) of pure rum, three gills of water, a splash of lemon, and a dash of sugar was given with noon dinner and evening supper.
- "Nancy Dawson," a fife-piped tune, signalled the noon ration.
- According to records of the time, naval and military rum issues can be dated from the capture of Port Royal (Annapolis Royal) in 1710 from the French inhabitants.

A RUM TALE (NOT FOR THE QUEASY)

After the Battle of Trafalgar (1805), a story goes that Lord Nelson's body was submerged for preservation in a barrel of ship's rum. When Nelson's crew caught wind of this, they partook of the "full-bodied" spirit. Grog afterward was referred to in certain quarters as "Nelson's Blood." New meaning to the expression "dead drunk" ensued.

DID RUM DERIVE ITS NAME FROM "RUMBULLION"? SOME ALTERNATIVE CLAIMS:

- Dutch seafarers' large drinking glasses were called "rummers"
- Latin for sugar: *saccharum* (emphasis on the last syllable)
- French for aroma: *arome* (pronounced "ahh-rummm")

Other merchants, pirates, and English imbibers were drinking:

- ⇨ bumboo—rum with water, sugar, and nutmeg
- ⇨ rum punch (derived from the Hindustan word "panch" meaning "five"), a mixed drink made of rum, tea, sugar, lemon, and cinnamon (which went a long way to nullifying rum's acrid taste)

UP SPIRITS, GROG TOTS, AND THE CANADIAN NAVY

From its foundation in 1910, the Royal Canadian Navy parroted virtually all of the traditional Royal Navy trappings, including the grog ration. Recruiters coyly promised travel and rum with a view.

The rum issue drill was a rigidly traditional and formal procedure. At 1100 hours, "Up Spirits" was piped. The tot team—a witnessing officer, a regulating petty officer or master-at-arms, and a supply rating, starched with purpose, entered the spirit room or locker. The spirit room was a compartment in a ship's bowels with locks and a flooding system as a safety measure in light of "rum's explosive nature and its alluring attractiveness to fun-loving sailors." Rum was pumped from barrels into a small keg that could hold a day's ration. The tot team proceeded with said keg to an upper deck or "any sheltered position in readiness for the rum/grog issue." A perk of NCOs, the chief and petty officer's messmen, permitted these members of the tot team to draw first ration. The crew's ration consisted of two parts water to one part rum, or a sailor could appear before the Witnessing Officer to have his rum added to either water or a soft drink at a ratio of 1:2. Only RCN sailors over twenty years old could draw a rum ration.

But what about abstainers (gasp, surely these didn't exist in the services)? Retired navy captain Max Reid weighed in on this issue: "Those abstainers were given a few cents per day [twenty-five cents in the 1960s] in lieu of rum. These temperates were labeled 'T' on the ship's books and Leave/Station card. A 'T' was also branded a 'Kill-Joy' for not contributing into the communal pot for such occasions as birthdays, promos etcetera."

RUM AND MESS IN THE RCN

For cheer on long voyages, for surviving extreme weather bombs, and for strengthening that all-important naval fighting spirit, rum stood ready for sailors. Rum rations and chow co-existed like hulls and water, or meals and the mess, the shipboard refuge from tough daily duty that served as the centre of a sailor's life at sea.

Some reasons why the mess was the favoured deck

- The mess was the one—the only for that matter—actual social club for crewmembers.
- It was the locale for the highlight of their arduous days, noon dinner.
- The grog issue took place in the mess.

Cook-of-the-mess rules

- Cook-of-the-mess was a rotational duty for each and every mess member.
- Duties: preparing the mess for meals, washing up the dishes, scrubbing out the mess, and drawing the rum.
- If grog was issued in the mess, the cook-of-the-mess or the leading hand of the mess played "mother" and got to pour the rum.

Arguments, sometimes inciting donnybrooks, erupted when the cook-of-the-mess attempted to get away with "shorting a ration," or intentionally spilling a few drops into a catch basin like a pot or mixing bowl. The idea was to be miserly, so that, in effect, there would be a few fingers of "gash" remaining to warm the cook-of-the-mess's thirsty (and bottomless) cockles.

By the 1960s, the end of the rum ration was in sight. Sailors had their status upgraded from "labourer" to "technician," which "precluded drinking on the job." Overnight leave and better pay set up longer shore life for sailors in housing provided by the Crown. As sailors' social lives became more land-based, the mess deck took on a decreased role. No more the crew's social epicentre, the need for naval rum dwindled. In 1970, the Royal Navy stopped issuing rum tots. A year later, the Canadian Navy followed suit. And with that, the navy practice of "Up Spirits" and its "upon-the-briny-seas-fellowship-connection" was summarily scuttled.

FACTORS ENCOURAGING A RELIANCE ON RUM IN THE YEARS 1764 TO 1850:

- a harsh environment
- illiteracy (can't read; can drink)
- poor transportation and communications links
- strenuous work (logging, fishing, trapping)
- the handy availability of cheap rum for social, recreational, festive, ceremonial, and medicinal purposes

HOW RUM POURED INTO NOVA SCOTIA

We all know pirates loved it. For one hundred percent proof you only have to check out the ear-to-ear grin creasing fabled jolly-rogering Captain Morgan's kisser on the label of a brand of Jamaican rum.

For some French, Dutch, and British colonialist businessmen then populating the New World, rum epitomized more than tavern fare for weekends in a free port. It meant business. Big trade business. Which, up and running, transformed the 1700s into boom years for ocean trade between the West Indies, England, Europe, and the American colonies. As commerce soared, so too did the popularity of rum as a beverage and trade commodity. Distilleries popped up across the pond, and discerning rum drinkers gave thumbs way up to the English product. The output of distilleries in Massachusetts and Rhode Island prompted this historical observation: "new England rum was vastly inferior to even the worst Caribbean rum. Its greatest adherents were those who couldn't afford a choice." In Nova Scotia, 1749 saw the creation of "Chebucto" on the skirt of one of the world's great harbours.

Shortly after, two significant conversions occured: Chebucto became Halifax in honour of George Dunk, the Earl of Halifax, Chief Lord of Trade and Plantations and the settlement's high-domed mastermind; Halifax became a major rum-distilling centre.

RUM TIMES IN NOVA SCOTIA: THE EARLY YEARS

From a report sent to the Britsh Lord Treasurer from Colonel Sam Vetch concerning provisions at Annapolis, December 14, 1711:

> "All provisions are very dear, particularly Rum, which must be instead of Beer, which the Severity of the winter freezes in that cold country."

A recipe for spruce beer from James Wolfe's superior officer, General Jeffery Amherst, writ large in 1759.

- ➪ Take 7 pounds of good spruce.
- ➪ Boil well tills [sic] the bark peels off.
- ➪ Take the spruce out and put 3 gallons of Molasses to the liquor.
- ➪ Boil again, scumming it well as it boils.
- ➪ Take it out of the kettle and put it in a cooler.
- ➪ Boil the remainder of the water sufficient for a Barrel of 30 gallons.
- ➪ When milkwarm in the cooler, put in a pint of Yest [sic] into it and mix well.
- ➪ Then put in the Barrel and let it work for 2 to 3 days.
- ➪ Keep filling it up as it works out.
- ➪ When done working, bung it up with a tent peg in the Barrel to give it vent every now and then.
- ➪ It may be used in 2 to 3 days and keeps a great well.

SOME OF RUM'S COMPETITION IN THE SETTLEMENTS

Settlers know that when certain common substances immersed in warm water in "just the right proportion" are left to their own devices long enough, alcohol will be manufactured.

The results: ale; malt beer; hop beer; bee's beer—like mead, which also uses fermented honey; buck beer—"North Shore Champagne"—strong brew, like a bock beer; spruce beer.

For over three hundred years, trade thrived between Nova Scotia and the West Indies. Molasses and rum were dealt for dried codfish, timber, and furs. In the early 1700s, Canso pulsed as a U.S. fishing station; it was a vital commercial outpost of the New England trade network. Importers shipped rum, a key commodity in the trade network, through the region to: New England; through the Straits of Canso to Tatamagouche, where overland transportation disperses the distillate to outlying Acadian settlements; the new French fortress at Louisbourg, where rum's popularity prompted the fort's Governor, Des Herbiers, to complain in 1749 about "the excessive use of alcohol by the forces."

CALIBOGUS: THE 1700S ACADIAN CURE FOR SCURVY

▶ what it is: an elixir of West Indies rum and home brew spruce beer

RUM AND THE EXPULSION OF 1755

The Treaty of Utrecht (1713) compelled the French to cede mainland Nova Scotia to Britain with the exception of Île Royale (Cape Breton). The Acadians, the predominant corps of regional inhabitants, were given a year to take an unqualified oath of allegiance. They refused, and their population flourished from approximately two thousand in 1710 to better than twelve thousand by 1750. Meanwhile, in England and Europe, yet another war broke out—the Seven Years' War. With England and France at daggers drawn, the local Brits began to look askance at the Île Royale French, who easily outnumbered the English claque of merchants, fishermen, and a handful of troops. English disquiet was intensified, egged on by anti-British sentiments transmitted into Acadian and Mi'kmaq hearts and minds by incendiary French missionary Abbé Jean-Louis Le Loutre. When a last-chance take-it-or-leave-it oath of allegiance ultimatum was roundly rejected, the Brits decided to handle the perceived danger with blunt force. And conveniently, the rum trade provided an excuse for an attack.

Indeed, one of the Expulsion's first acts, the sacking of Tatamagouche, was a blatant attempt to cut trade between Louisbourg and the Acadian settlements along the Minas Basin. British leadership made rum an incentive for British troops to carry out the 1755 Expulsion. From the journal of Abijah Willard, August 16:

> "I went with a Small party of men over a large River Tatamagoush wher I Burnt 12 Buildings one of which was a Storehouse with Rum and Malosas and Iron ware and another Rum sugar and molasas and wine. A Masshouse I ordered the men to Draw as much Rum as they had Bottles to Cary which they Did and set fire to the rest."

SNAPSHOTS OF EIGHTEENTH- AND NINETEENTH-CENTURY HALIFAX: RUM'S KIND OF TOWN

- ➪ Halifax Reverend James MacGregor, sizing up the rumbullian scene, despaired: "The business of one-half of the people was to sell rum, the other half to drink it."
- ➪ A shocked and appalled critic in 1862 complained: "So abundant is liquor sold in forms of strong drink in Halifax that the city is nothing less than a great big Rum shop. Rum on the right hand, and rum on the left; rum before you, rum behind you, and rum all around you."
- ➪ Government incentives offered an impetus for rum entrepreneuring, hoping settlers would jump into some aspect of the lucrative rum trade. A rum allowance was given, amounting to three-and-one-quarter gallons per head in the first year. This proved way too modest. Amazingly, imports exceeded that supply when per capita consumption soared to twelve gallons per annum.

Dealing rum achieved liftoff as a major Halifax business enterprise. George Hick, a one-time blacksmith turned rum dealer, posted a letter dated November 30, 1749, to his wife residing in England:

> "I being set up for myself (in the rum business), keeps a man at work with me, and pays him 7 shillings a week from Matinmas till candlemas. I sell rum by the quart, and in smaller quantities, and lays out 2 guineas a week in it, by which I find I get money very fast."

Rum sold by publicans and licenced merchants reached the ever-thirsty in a variety of amounts: by the pint, by the quart in black glass bottles, and in five- or ten-gallon kegs.

A PECKING ORDER OF RUM

- ➪ Premium price: top-of-the-line Jamaican rum notable for its superior strength and flavour. Savvy Jamaican rum producers double-distilled all the molasses to withdraw excess water and to boost their product's alcohol content.
- ➪ Mid-range: Grenada and Antigua double-distilled rums.
- ➪ Cheap and cheaper: Barbados and Nevs throat scorchers.
- ➪ Liquid barnacle removers: New England rum, and shockingly, dear ol' Nova Scotia rum.

There were, of course, other alcoholic beverages available for drinkers in the eighteenth and nineteenth centuries. Brandy and gin (a.k.a. "geneva") were popular with New Brunswickers flush with heavy coin. However, "geneva" rated low in Halifax rum joints. Statistics showed that rum consumption exceeded brandy, whisky, and gin combined, three times over. Beer was on tap but flowed in paltry amounts. Whisky itself did nothing-to-crow-about business until very late in the century. Why, you ask? Price. Rum was the thirst-quencher of choice in Halifax because it was the cheapest.

Rum drawn from a keg atop the tavern bar was served neat (i.e. straight) to customers by the gill (one-quarter of a pint) or by the half-gill if they were driving—horses, that is.

Every innkeeper or barkeep had their own special rum concoctions, happily dispensed by the pint and quart: hot water, rum, and molasses drinks called "flips," and the reliable Acadian rum and spruce beer combo, calibogus.

In the 1700s, labourers took rum breaks from work at 11:00 a.m. and 4:00 p.m. Often workers were paid in rum. Construction contracts even stipulated rum be provided. Labour was known to put down tools and effect a sitdown if the rum provision failed to put in an appearance.

Rum even influenced labour negotiations. In exchange for sobriety on the job site, Joseph Salter wharf workers won a shorter workday, and thereby, more downtime for rum.

MIGHTY MAUGER'S WORLD

Joshua Mauger (1725–1788): sea captain, Royal Navalist, privateer, slave trader, smuggler, vitctualer (grocer), merchant, distiller, lobbyist, British Member of Parliament, and Agent-General for Nova Scotia.

In the opinion of Colonel Edward Cornwallis, "Mauger is clearly engaged in illicit and contraband trade. He's a kingpin of the illicit trade between Halifax and Louisbourg." Despite hostile relations between the French and English in Nova Scotia, Mauger played both sides fast and loose for big commercial gains. As the largest shipowner in Halifax between 1749 and 1760, he used his vessels to run produce up to French-controlled Louisbourg and even brokered deals between the French and the Mi'kmaq for French-made tomahawks and scalping knives, which were in turn used against the British.

Cornwallis also took time to denounce Mauger to the imperial government in London, singling him out as "an audacious smuggler if not worse." Cornwallis went on to wonder why "so dubious a person should be permitted to act as Agent-Victualer for Nova Scotia."

In his capacity as a wheeler and a dealer, Mauger was the go-to guy if you had "something to trade from influence to furs." "For eleven years," a chronicler stated, "if anyone in Nova Scotia had something to sell, or something to buy, Joshua Mauger was the man to look up."

Around 1749, Jersey sea captain Joshua Mauger, age twenty-four, moved to Halifax from Louisburg, where he had done so-so business as a merchant. His intention? To become stinkin' rich. His timing to be in Halifax in that particular year couldn't have been better. Government money was flowing to underwrite development of an entrepreneurial class. No small thanks to the intercession of pals in high places back in London, in 1749 Mauger received an appointment as Agent-Victualer to the Royal Navy in Halifax, meaning he supplied food provisions to the fleet. With the navy as a steady client, Mauger opened several provisions shops in downtown Halifax, on McNab's Island, as well as at Piziquid, Minas, Grand Pré, and Annapolis. Mauger lost his lofty title of Agent-Victualer when he barred investigating authorities, acting on suspicion that the building contained smuggled goods, admittance to one of his warehouses. Because smuggling and Mauger went together like wet and water, the likelihood the authorities were correct in their assumption was as sure as day follows night. Was it a crippling career-ender? For a player as conniving and canny as Mauger, hardly. Well-acquainted with the favoured place of rum in the navy (in which he served as a youth), the ever-cunning opportunist opened his first Halifax rum distillery (the first of two) in 1751 and finessed for himself the

position of chief supplier of Nova Scotia rum issued to military personnel in the local garrisons and navy yard.

Smuggled molasses underpinned Mauger's growing liquor enterprise. With the Seven Years' War messing with international trade rules, rum-making supplies were difficult to secure. Nova Scotia vessels routinely voyaged to French- or Dutch-controlled Caribbean islands with ladings of salt cod, furs, and forestry products, which off-loaded there for return cargoes of sugar and molasses.

Ethics on idle, Mauger took possession of a landing of 17,250 gallons of Grand Terre molasses listed on the waybill as "British Plant Produce." No small wonder that wily Mauger got rich. And with enormous wealth came, scant surprise, political influence, which Mauger's contemporaries dubbed his "coils of mystifying connections." Mauger's tentacles soon reached as far as London, England. Compelled to do his bidding, the first Nova Scotia legislative council protected Mauger's distilling interests by levying a five-pence per gallon duty on all imported rum. Mauger also had his hooks into the Halifax custom house, which nestled, comfortingly for Mauger, in his "sphere of control." Ditto the Canso custom office, where Mauger's clout provided a stunning example of his inordinate and virtually unassailable power. Mauger's Canso custom office associate, naval officer Jonathan Binney, found himself under investigation for "irregularities found in

TOP THREE VIOLATIONS BY LIQUOR HOUSES WARRANTING PROSECUTION:

- ▶ Selling liquor on a Sunday.
- ▶ Being open after 11:00 p.m. closing.
- ▶ Countenancing disorderliness on the premises.

Canso shipping records." The presiding Governor Legge ordered the arrest of Binney, jailing him, his wife, and his children. But it was truly a mug's game to cross Mauger. Angry, Mauger leant his substantial political heft on officials, demanding Binney and his family's release and a significant reduction in the charges. The officials caved, meeting Mauger's demands. But he was not through. London, to Governor Legge's surprise and dismay, recalled him. His Nova Scotia business in good hands (with his trusted lieutenants), Mauger sailed back to Britain. Hardly a neophyte at backroom politics, Mauger decided to run in an election as a Member of Parliament. He succeeded, of course, as the member for Poole from 1768 to 1780. The Colossus of Rum's foremost legacy in Nova Scotia? Mauger's powerful provincial business and political connections firmly secured Nova Scotia's loyalty during the American Revolution.

A SOBERING NOTE FROM HELEN CREIGHTON'S BOOK, *BLUENOSE MAGIC*

"To cure a man of drink, take an eel and put it in rum, but don't leave the eel in long enough to die. Then give the rum to the person to drink. But don't tell him about the eel. If he drinks it, he will never touch rum again."

RUM AND THE FAT CITY LIFE OF EARLY NINETEENTH CENTURY NOVA SCOTIA

In 1808, protectionistic Americans slapped an embargo on British produce. In retaliation, Britain declared Halifax and Shelburne free ports. The ports thrived as clearing houses for European, Caribbean, and American goods.

- ⇨ Nova Scotian shippers grabbed a sizeable chunk of the eastern seaboard trade, and rum flowed freely.
- ⇨ Drinking became a fundamental feature of daily life. A prerequisite for a successful business career was a vendor's licence to peddle liquor. Obtaining one was easier than falling down.
- ⇨ Taverns catering to travellers at ferry terminals and stage coach stops popped up all over.
- ⇨ The estimated number of businesses, houses, and shops selling liquor in 1860s Halifax: 200 to 300.
- ⇨ Number of drinking dens for every 100 people, factoring in women and children: 1
- ⇨ Percentage of licensed liquor dealers (with the exception of a restrictive period between the mid-1880s and mid-1890s) that were women: 10
- ⇨ Government's revenue accruing from custom duties on legally imported rum from Britain and the West Indies in the 1830s: 1/4 to 1/2 of total receipts.

A LICENCE TO SELL

"Licencees shall at all times, keep and maintain good order in the House, Shop or House of Entertainment for which such Licences shall be granted, and shall not suffer any Riot, Disturbance, or Breach of the Peace therein, nor any Raffle or Raffles, nor the using or Playing of any kind of Game Or Games, by Dice, Cards or Otherwise, therein on pain of forfeiture of Licence."

Prosecution of unlicensed booze merchants hinged on proof "that bottles, or decanters, or tumblers, or glasses, or other vessels, which are usually employed for holding and using liquor, were found in and upon the premises of such accused party, and had recently been used."

A LEG OVER FOR A COMPETITIVE LEG UP

In the 1870s, a glut of "marginal rum shops" forced tavern owners to "throw in a little extra for John Thomas" and rely on prostitution as a source of revenue, an area of service typically overseen by the wife of the tavern owner. Henrietta McKegney, a server employed by bar owner Isaac Sallis, testified in court on two occasions in 1859 that "Mrs. Sallis took from her, a dollar as bed rental."

"Prostitution," it was said of grog joints in the 1870s, "gave the worst liquor shops their bad name."

From Halifax lawyer/writer R. H. Dana Junior—author of *Two Years Before the Mast*:

> Donned blue loose trousers, rough jacket and glased [sic] cap, and set out for a cruise about the town. Below the barracks, saw about a half a dozen houses, in each of which a fiddle, with tambourines or triangles, was playing, and a

crowd of the lowest description. Both males and females were going in and out ... Buttoning up my coat and pulling my cap over my face, I went into the largest of these houses. The entry terminated in an oblong room with low and black walls, sanded floor and closely barred shutters, used as a dancing hall. At one end was a platform holding two chairs upon which the fiddle and the triangle players sat. At the other end was the bar, at which the bloated, red-faced master of the house sold glasses of rum, brandy and wine to the girls and their partners. In the middle of the room, in an armchair, sat the old harradan [sic], the "mother" of the house, with a keen wicked eye, looking sharp after the girls and seeing to it they made all the men dance and pay the fiddler and treat them at the bar after each dance.

CAUTIONARY LYRICS FROM A BALLAD OF THE TIMES

You sailors all, come lend an ear,
Come listen to my song
A trick of late was played on me,
It won't detain you long.
I came from sea the other day,
A girl I chanced to meet,
My friends will be expecting me
To dance on Barrack Street.
At eight o'clock that evening
The drinking did begin.
And when all hands had got their fill
The dancing did begin.

Me and my love danced all around
Unto a merry tune
When she says, "Dear, we will retire
To a chamber all alone."
The dancing being over,
To bed we did repair.
And there I fell fast asleep,
The truth I will declare.
My darling with me thirty pounds,
Gold watch and chain had fled,
And left me here, poor Jack alone,
Left naked in the bed.
Come, all you young sailor lads
A warning take by me.
Be sure and choose your company
When you go on a spree.
Be sure keep out of Barrack Street,
Or else you'll rue the day
With a woman's shirt and apron
They'll rig you out for sea.

THROUGH A RUM GLASS DARKLY

Tenement dwellers, soldiers in barracks, and sailors hit taverns for the warmth and as a swell party place for their favourite plebian divertissements. If a publican or barkeep in an illicit rum shop refused to serve a patron a drink for whatever reason, that person could buy a bottle therein and vamoose to any nearby dark alley, wharf, yard, or cemetery to guzzle.

SOLDIERS, SAILORS, DRINKERS, RAILERS

In the 1850s, Halifax's garrison of redcoats suffered through a period of abject idleness. The navy's Jack Tars fared no better. For all intents and purposes, military boys—their blood up and looking for some form of action—found plenty to choose from in the grog shops, brothels, and illicit rum shops on "Knock 'Em Down Row": Barrack Street (now Brunswick Street) and Albemarle Street (now Market Street). Waterfront dives farther down toward the harbour beckoned, often inhabited by thirsty visiting naval and merchant sailors (whose shipboard rules forbade alcohol consumption).

SOME EXCUSES FOR WHY SOLDIERS BEHAVED BADLY

⇨ Most were rough lads from the bottom rung of British society.

⇨ Often unwitting recruits got "drafted for service" by thuggish press gangs.

⇨ Commanding officers loathed them.

⇨ Lousy food.

⇨ Brutal discipline at the hands of disagreeable commanding officers.

⇨ Exorbitant prices gouged them at grog shops and brothels.

⇨ Vicious punishment inflicted on them following incidents of theft, assault, and looting.

INTIMATIONS OF TROUBLE AHEAD FOR "DEMON RUM"

For the rum-fuelled military, civilian law held little sway. Civilian developers, bent on establishing Halifax as a "well-ordered urban society," stewed in frustration. The seeds of temperance began to germinate.

- ➪ 1838 and 1850. Halifax. Four major disturbances flared up when military personnel avenged a colleague either beaten by an overly aggressive pimp or wasted from drinking tainted whorehouse rum.
- ➪ 1863. Brawls and excessive public drunkenness resulted in a brusque military edict ruling Barrack Street out-of-bounds to soldiers. Barrack Street shifted into a no-go zone lasting for years.
- ➪ June 1874. A ferocious dust-up among sailors and soldiers forced military authorities to ban personnel from Albemarle Street and Barrack Street unequivocally. Soldiers retreated to the less public refuge of their canteens.
- ➪ The rum ration and "beer money," standard army practices, terminated in the 1860s.
- ➪ Military brass now included temperance boys with knickers in a knot over "maintaining good relations between town and garrison." Meanwhile, Halifax continued to flaunt the approbation as "the Gibraltar of the rum trade."

AN ADDRESS TO A JUG OF RUM CIRCA 1854

Here only by a cook controlled
And slender walls of earthen mold,
In all the pomp of death, repose
The seeds of many a bloody nose;
The fist for fighting; nothing loath;
The passion which no word can tame,
That bursts like sulphur into flame;
Nose carbuncled, glowing red;
The bloated eye, the broken head;
The tree that bore the deadly fruit,
Of murder, maiming and dispute,
The images of gloomy jail;
The giddy thought on mischief bent;
The midnight hour in riot spent;
All these within this jug appear;
And Jack the Hangman in the rear.

RUM AND LIVERPOOL

⇨ From the 1760s to the 1820s, Liverpool, Nova Scotia, provided berths for shippers (rum by now a familiar commodity); fishers, who, in a couple of runs per year, caught northern cod off Labrador; and the Royal Navy. All were manned by sailors with unquenchable thirsts and willing throats.

⇨ From the settlement's founding in 1759, the rum trade fuelled Liverpool's primary industry, the fishery, supplying barter goods to exchange for the many import products the settlement needed.

- ⇨ Rum doubled as compensation for hard, hazardous, and discomforting daily toil. Loggers and agricultural workers accepted dark rum as their pay packet.
- ⇨ By the late eighteenth century, Liverpool had evolved into a wild, openly libertine and intemperate burg.
- ⇨ Merchant groups, vessel owners, and adventurers—sometimes involved in privateering and smuggling—ran the economy. The presence of the Royal Navy struck them as either a business opportunity or a threat to the darker aspects of their local enterprise.
- ⇨ Smugglers showed a deep dislike for customs officials. By 1820 the rap on Nova Scotians was that they were incorrigible dodgers of paying duties to the excise department—particularly on imports of rum and sugar.
- ⇨ Pleas arose from concerned citizens and church groups for temperance. They agreed to moderate consumption of beer, ales, and wines, but sternly drew the line at spirits (i.e. rum).

HOLY HOUSES AGAINST LIQUOR

1) Baptists
2) Methodists
3) Congregationalists
4) Presbyterians
5) Scottish/Irish Catholics

The top ten list of others opposed to alcohol use

1) rural farmers
2) merchants

3) middle-class professionals
4) artisans (go figure)
5) doctors
6) lawyers
7) politicians
8) schoolteachers
9) civil servants
10) writers (go figure again)

The temperance movement in Liverpool grew as the destructive roistering effects of rum on the sensibilities of local lads took a toll on community civility. By 1838, Liverpudlian discontent focused on "the state of affairs in a town which made much of its income from the sale and importation of Rum." Heartset on entrenching a proper code of behaviour, evangelical church leaders to sea captains rallied to the temperance cause and spoiled for a fight. Some caught up in the reformist zeal zoomed beyond the original moderation dictum and yowled for out-and-out abstinence from each and every intoxicating beverage—without exception. Because the temperance demand cut to the core of Anglican ritual (sacramental wine was used for the Eucharist), the Anglican Church passed. Nevertheless, dogged temperance folk

A DICTIONARY DEFINITION: TEMPERANCE

▶ the state or quality of being temperant; self-restraint in conduct, expression, indulgence of the appetites; moderation

▶ moderation in drinking alcoholic liquors or total abstinence from alcoholic liquors pressed Anglican rectors to reconsider. With genteel politesse, the Anglican clerics demured.

Three watchwords of temperance

1) Love
2) Purity
3) Fidelity

In the middle of the nineteenth century, temperance societies peppered Nova Scotia, due in part to well-organized members of the privileged elite with eloquent oratory skills bolstered with financial and political clout. In the 1850s, Leonard Tilley (before becoming a premier of New Brunswick and a Father of Confederation) served as Most Worthy Patriarch of the Sons of Temperance for all of North America.

What were Temperance Society meetings like? At the grassroots level, meetings appeared more social than fire-snortingly political. They aped secretive Freemason meetings. Consider that members:

- ⇨ dressed up in society regalia;
- ⇨ whispered passwords to gain entry; and
- ⇨ organized a hierarchy of grand worthy patriarchs, scribes, chaplins, and sentinels.

TEMPERANCE MEETING PROGRAMMING

- ⇨ Songs: Hacks grafted worthy news events to popular broadside ballads to musically chronicle demon rum's dastardly part in murders most foul and other related villainy:

"If I ever gain my Liberty
That enemy I will shun.
Steet walking and bad company
And likewise drinking rum."

- Poetry and poesy reading.
- Scary and cautionary storytelling such as this gem from the minutes of a temperance meeting:

  "The way you drink liquor from the money you get is the way you'll drink fire and Brimstone in Hell."

- Soul-stirring narrations of miraculous reform versus the grotesque deaths due to ardent spirits drinking, a favourite being "spontaneous combustion of rum-sodden derelicts," great tinder for alighting reformist souls ablaze.
- Debates on abstinence that fall off the subject to argue the pros and cons of topics such as: "Which is clam digging? Fishing or farming?"
- Tea, cakes, juice, or cider (before fermentation, of course).

Also at temperance meetings:

- disputes over philosophical and tactical ploys on winning the battle of minds for total abstinence (i.e. moral persuasion versus legislation);
- arguments pro and con on leniency for society members whose livelihoods depend on rum—temperance (dry) ship owners and captains of vessels shipping rum; and
- heated accusations of hypocrisy among certain members and charges of pledge-breaking.

A society meeting debates a thorny pledge issue

First, the sticky situation: a sea captain and temperance man was offered a lucrative contract to ship a cargo of rum. If he adhered strictly to society code and turned down the offer, he would be financially adrift upon the proverbial high seas without a rudder.

Now, the solution: the Temperance Society advised him to accept the contract but to decline "receiving commission or pay in intoxicating liquor."

Social scientists could rightly point out that this adjustment to the "rule" spoke to an innate character trait of Nova Scotians; that is, to choose practicality and expediency over dogma. This mindset played a formidable role when the American temperance absolutist F. W. Kellogg and his Sons of Temperance arrived.

TWO RUM-RELATED FACTORS THAT HARDEN TEMPERANCE RESOLVE

- ▶ Waterfront and back-alley rum shop dens, brothels, and "spirited" brawling.
- ▶ Sordid and depraved practices such as slave trading and piracy.

AND NOW FOR SOMETHING COMPLETELY DISSENTIOUS...

South Rawdon's partially built Temperance Hall burned down thanks to local temperance opponents who thought first to vandalize the structure before torching it. Such overt acts of opposition aside, in the years between 1820 and 1870, temperance movement pressure, at both a social and political level, reduced Liverpool's "filthy lucrative" rum trade from a torrent to a trickle.

The temperance press: selected listings

- ⇨ redemption speeches of reclaimed drunkards
- ⇨ nuggets of wisdom: "Intemperance has been a great architect for it builds prisons, almshouses and hospitals."
- ⇨ literary turns:

"I met an aged man, a man of cares,
Wrinkled and carved and white with hoary hairs
Rum is the tyrant of the soul, he said
Ye young and fair, take warning from the dead."

Op-ed commentary (as it was published):

"A Curious Comparison

Matrimony is like rum punch, man is the rum. Sharp and violent; woman the sweet and dissolving love the boiling water, which grows in time quite cold. The wedding day is therefore a most important epoch in human life for both parties. With closed eyes they chose a brewed bumper, filled with happiness or misery and must drink it to the bottom. Man standing at the alter, gives up a great deal of his liberty and his privileges, and the woman gains them; and such restriction of the rights of the former expands that of the latter."

A few words from Willie Dennis, temperance man and future owner of the Halifax *Herald*, in 1875:

"Every organization to succeed must command a press. To an Order a more useful agent cannot be found. A newspaper will do more good than a public meeting—more good than our Lodge meetings. It does what our Lodges

> and divisions fail to do—moves its missions work with the precision, facility and power of a machine."

The "Rum Press" patricians, infuriated by the plebian penchant to readily engage in drinking bouts and dance partnered with rum, took upon their moralist shoulders the burden of protecting society's lesser individuals from themselves. Detailed stories, often tabloid-lurid and "augmented" for impact, spotlighted the drink trade's most squalid and reprehensible sides. One crusading broadsheet, aptly named the *Watchman*, identified for its appalled readership the locations of illicit dives and, for kickers, tallies of the number of stiffs littering alleys off Halifax's Brunswick Street. More often than not, such narrow and single-themed publishing found its sales potential limited. One classic example was the fate of Firman McClure, the Truro-based publisher of the *Temperance Index*. Here's a taste of McClure from January 2, 1891:

> "The Index is a sworn enemy of the saloon, not because it would claim any right to dictate to men what they shall eat or drink, but because the saloon is an institution that is at variance with the peace and parity of the home and an enemy of all influences aimed to elevate individuals."

In December 1892, because so few temperance supporters subscribed to his broadsheet, both the index "gasrag" and McClure lost fiscal buoyancy and, humiliatingly, sank from sight.

THE YANKEE "COLD WATER ARMY" INVASION OF 1848

Total abstinence groups in Nova Scotia invited American abstinence crusader F. W. Kellogg and his Sons of Temperance to present inspirational lectures and instruction on the techniques of gung-ho Yankee temperance politics. Kellogg advocated setting up youth groups to:

- ⇨ convince their parents to take the pledge;
- ⇨ form singing groups to warble uplifting melodies that extol the sacred virtues of sobriety.

Temperance adherents were encouraged by Kellogg to inundate local press with messages on drunkenness and its ties to Beelzebub, and to pressure politicians to cast off any aspects of reasonability and replace them with zealotry.

Kellogg's tactics:

- ⇨ campaign like a military organization;
- ⇨ run meetings like a religious revival meeting complete with a temperance choir belting out fiery redemptive temperance songs;
- ⇨ increase membership with craftily planned programs of music, entertainment, and fellowship.

The initial enthusiasm for Kellogg's near-fascist, in-your-face abstinence-crusading proved to be a hard sell, even among diehard abstinence society members. Returning to give a talk to the Queen's

County Total Abstinence Society in 1849, Kellog discovered that, in the space of a year, a seismic shift in opinion as to the aptness of his directives had decreased the initial groundswell of popular support for his "Cold Water Army." No longer was there blind obeisance from members. From the minutes book of the Queen's County Total Abstinence Society:

> "There was decided opposition from some of the officers of the Total Abstinence Society on the grounds that he [Kellogg] was a 'Son of Temperance' and they refused to attend the meeting that they were as full of temperance as they could hold and that he nor any one else could teach them ought [sic]."

Undaunted and stoked with righteous fervor, Kellogg continued the battle. Rum dealers and traders remained ugly blights, rife for consignment to eternal perdition. It was not for Kellogg to shirk his divine duty. "For the triumph of evil," he flintily snorted, "it is only necessary that good men do nothing." Assailed by unrelenting temperance arguments, the rum trade took a double hit—commercially and socially. To pass as a decent and responsible progressive in the 1850s and '60s in the eyes of one's peers meant siding with the "drys." Hectoring politicians for an out-and-out ban on liquor trafficking and the implementation of total abstinence at last found receptive ears. Taking a cue from the Maine Prohibition Act of 1851, prohibition legislation passed in New Brunswick in 1855.

Simultaneously, the influence of the Total Abstinence Society and the Sons of Temperance in New Brunswick and in Nova Scotia paradoxically decreased. A year later, a newly elected New Brunswick government concluded that, by gad, the prohibition law would dry up a substantial and vital government revenue stream, so the New Brunswick prohibition legislation was abolished.

Meanwhile, across the provincial border, no less than five prohibition drives forced an attempt to install similar legislation in Nova Scotia.

THE FEDS ENTER THE FRAY

In 1878 the Dunking Act (also known as the Scott Act or Canada Temperance Act) became a statute. Hereby, "If one quarter of the electors of any municipal unit request a vote by petition and, if in the resulting election, the Canada Temperance Act is favoured by a simple majority, then no liquor can be sold in that area except for

- ⇨ medicinal purposes
- ⇨ sacramental purposes
- ⇨ industrial purposes.

A decision can only be reversed by a similar election to be held every three years."

As a result of the Temperance Act:

- ⇨ Most localities voted for abstinence. Cumberland County, for example, remained "Scott dry" for thirty years.
- ⇨ A patchwork-quilt pattern of dry, dry, dry, wet, dry, dry, dry localities blanketed the province. The Scott Act was replaced in 1910 by a Nova Scotia prohibition act.
- ⇨ "Ever-thirsties" residing in a dry area "went next door" to a wet area for a beaker, bottle, or belt of booze.
- ⇨ Provincially, Nova Scotia went "bone dry" from 1916 to 1929—the year the Temperance Act was abandoned federally.
- ⇨ Before 1929, the Act's "wet" exception was Halifax.

OFF ROAD AND TRACK IN "BONE DRY" COUNTRY

- ➪ A tavern ledger of John Sargent and Son held in the collection of the Cape Sable Historical Society—a community known for not issuing a liquor licence in over one hundred years—undercuts the notion of strict adherence to abstinence.
- ➪ King's College students frequented the taverns in Windsor and responded to college vice-president William Cochan's anti-drinking disciplinary measures by trashing his lecture room.
- ➪ Found in a letter dated June 30, 1895, from James W. Edwards to the Honourable William MacDonald: "The new hotel is running at full blast. It is a mistake to call it a hotel. I cannot call it anything but a big rum shop. The whisky has a great flavour, I believe, hence the Liberal patronage."
- ➪ In "dry" localities, fruitcakes laced with rum, rum cakes, and rum balls increase in popularity and frequency.

SEMI-OPEN IN NEW GLASGOW

The 1878 Scott Act made selling grog illegal. Still, open bars remained a fact of life in New Glasgow until 1910. Until 1930, bars were classified as "semi-opens," and legitimate liquor sellers found themselves re-classified as illicit bootleggers.

"Cover shops," such as general stores, sold rum under-the-counter; various dives and blind pigs (unlicensed liquor joints) also catered to the "ever-thirsty." Law enforcement, at best inadequate, adopted a "why make a fuss" attitude, limiting raids and arrests to cases not likely to impede the profit margins of the local underground economy.

HAPPENINGS IN HALIFAX, A.K.A. "THE GIBRALTAR OF THE RUM TRADE"

- ⇨ Military reforms marked a transition from King Rum to beer and ales as standard canteen issue.
- ⇨ Temperance crusaders, butting up against bootleggers and unlicensed rum sellers, attempted the exorcism of what the Abstainer dubbed "the curse of the city."
- ⇨ Temperance society members perpetuated a myth that "alcohol abuse is a problem of the working class."
- ⇨ Legislators attempted to prevent publicans from "providing entertainment in their establishments."
- ⇨ Targeted frivolities were skittles, board games, and dancing.
- ⇨ The high-minded opinion: "If the poor were going to drink, they could damn well do so in boring and austere surroundings."
- ⇨ Taverns after 1886 became "pale reflections of the legitimate rum shops or houses of entertainment."

The gain: improved morality and social order.
The loss: the working class were dispossessed of a vital social outlet.

THE MISCONDUCTING OF COUNTY ELECTIONS

Because county elections stretched over several weeks, the process was open territory for corruption and abuse. Fisticuffs, bribery, and rampant drunkenness marred any vestige of civility the electoral system might have boasted of. In the 1793 election, for as long as the Halifax polls stayed open, candidates ran open houses (a.k.a. houses of entertainment) providing electors with lodgings, stabling, grub, and plenty of rum prior to voting.

Buying and selling democracy, 1867 to 1874 style
(from a newspaper article by Stephen Kimber)

- ⇨ outside a polling station, a party worker collars a voter
- ⇨ voter agrees to sell his vote for a reward
- ⇨ voter takes a ballot pre-marked for a certain candidate
- ⇨ voter enters the polling station and is handed a blank ballot
- ⇨ voter slips into a voting booth and does nothing
- ⇨ voter emerges and hands the poll captain the pre-marked ballot
- ⇨ outside, voter hands over the blank ballot to the party worker
- ⇨ voter trots off happily with a bottle of rum tucked under an arm
- ⇨ process repeats itself until the polls close
- ⇨ the secret ballot was introduced in 1870 to bring some order to elections

ANONYMOUS EDITORIAL COMMENT:

"The Rum-Drunkard, of all Drunkards, is the worst."

LAST KICK AT THE KEG AND THE RISE OF RUM SMUGGLING

Shifting tides of public opinion and fashion put rum's four-century run of influence on Nova Scotia's socio-economic makeup on the wane. Prohibition in the U.S. gave rum a last, short-lived frisson of outlaw excitement before the ardent spirit scaled back to the role it currently maintains and enjoys.

Prohibition 1918 to 1933: the Rum Row years

- Just as the United States entered its national prohibition years in 1920, Canadians made ready to chuck out their prohibition legislation.
- By 1926, Maritimers were tiring of prohibition, which, as they saw it, only made sense for smugglers, rumrunners, and bootleggers.
- 1929: Nova Scotia threw in the "drying" towel and joined the press, national politicos, and, yes, even clergymen in rebranding the "great experiment" the "dismal failure"—a policy

THE SHALLOW END OF THE VOTING POOL 1700–1850

- Men who owned a dwelling house or one hundred acres of land could vote (women wouldn't win voting rights until 1918).
- Fines for fraudulent voting in 1839:
  1) twenty-pound fine
  2) loss of property
- Those with nothing to lose were open to bribes of tobacco, clothing, and of course, rum.

success only if your game was to foster hypocrisy, corruption, and lawlessness.

- Only strict prohibitionists and rumrunners wept when Prohibition went south.

BACK IN NOVA SCOTIA, BAD NEWS LED TO OPPORTUNITY

- A catastrophic downturn in the fisheries and other traditional industries shook the economic footing of coastal communities dependent upon them.
- U.S. protectionist regulations restricted Nova Scotian fishers from directly landing catches in U.S. ports.
- Desperate fishers turned to "bottle fishing" to make ends meet. Clement Hiltz, former Lunenburg rum-runner, told *Maclean's* magazine's John Dermont: "I could make more money running one load of booze than I could in a year on the fishing boats." At fifteen Hiltz joined seven others to run rum aboard *Silver Arrow*, a re-purposed fishing schooner.
- Hiltz crewed on six rum-smuggling trips before returning to fishing. "It was scary out there.

IN THE USA

- It's legal to drink but a no-no to purchase or sell spirits.
- The P. T. Barnum Clever Idea Award for getting around prohibition restrictions goes to the sharpies that charged admission to see an awesome marvel and get a free drink in the bargain.

I don't know who we were more worried about; the coast guard cutters or the gangsters on Rum Row who wanted to hijack our load."

- ⇨ January 1925: *Maritime Merchant* calculated that about fifty vessels of Lunenburg's one-hundred-vessel fishing fleet engaged in the rum trade.
- ⇨ American "import syndicates" leased many vessels at the going rate of $2,500 per month, which inflated to $4,000 per month when U.S. enforcement upped its interdiction game.
- ⇨ Illicit booze shipped to Maine was, for the most part, all high-quality name-brand stock from British and European distilleries.
- ⇨ Public sympathies lay with the rum-runners, noble do-gooders all, risking everything to provide an, umm, essential service.
- ⇨ The "retail rum trade" (a.k.a. bootlegging) in the 1920s played a valuable welfare role, in particular for single mothers.

- ⇨ Bootleggers with dependent children often escaped imprisonment when arrested. Case in point, bootlegger Mrs. Donnie Hart of Saint John, arrested every year from 1916 to 1924, ducked stretches of hard time in the slammer thanks to her three, often bewildered but useful, kids.
- ⇨ By comparison, consider the punishment for a bootlegging conviction in the 1700s:

  a) first offence—an hour in the stocks or the pillory
  b) second offence—twenty lashes

FROM SHOW TO BUSINESS

Pictou County's Amy Mason returned to Nova Scotia from a short sojourn in Hollywood as an actress and, with capital and initiative and a "willingness to brave the moral disapproval of the respectable community," parlayed all three into success in the business of rum distribution. Hooray for Hollywood!

MORE ON WOMEN'S WILES

- ⇨ Rum-runner Gordon Steven's wife used some of his cargo to create a scrumptious golden cake liberally laced with rich sweet rum, a cunning method of eluding authorities when delivering rum to customers. Her golden cake ingredient list: flour, butter, rum, a topping of pecans, coconut, and more rich, sweet rum.
- ⇨ In the 1930s, when smuggling bootlegged rum past police, runners stowed a rum keg beneath a woman's skirt as she sat on the delivery car's back seat. Lawmen, smugglers well knew, would not pry into a woman's undergarments.

A RUM EXCHANGE ON THE TRUE NATURE OF SIN

A Lunenburg member of Parliament, and owner of several schooners, in reported conversation with United Church cleric Reverend John Pringle:

> "Sin, Dr. Pringle, what is sin anyway?"
> "Sin," Dr. Pringle replied, "is rum-running."

WHEN UNWANTED COMPANY PUTS A VISIT

The schooner *I'm Alone*, built in Nova Scotia, specifically for the rum trade and capable of handling 2,800 cases of liquor, sailed into waters off Texas with a hooch cargo to offload. *I'm Alone's* skipper, Captain Randall, went bug-eyed when a new U.S. government cutter, *Wolcott*, clocked at eleven knots full throttle, steamed into view off-stern. *Wolcott* picketed *I'm Alone*. The cutter's captain marked the distance from shore as 10.8 miles (later to become a bone of contention) and then signalled *I'm Alone* to "heave to," or stop. To underline the order, the cutter's crew fired blanks at the schooner. Getting the message, *I'm Alone* pulled up. *Wolcott*'s boatswain, Frank Paul, boarded *I'm Alone* with Captain Randall's permission. When Paul rejoined his mates, *I'm*

Alone sheeted in, caught air, and sailed away. *Wolcott* gave chase. *I'm Alone*'s getaway continued overnight. When dawn broke and he was two hundred miles offshore, Randall's blood ran cold when he saw another pursuer had shown up. The U.S. cutter *Dexter* moved in to partner up with *Wolcott* in hot pursuit but *I'm Alone* continued to flee. Suddenly rounds of slugs pounded into the vessel from *Dexter*, brutally punching holes in the hull and sending the helpless schooner to the bottom. As *I'm Alone* slipped beneath the waves, a French crewmember drowned. Anger over the incident from Canada, Britain, and France was quick and sharp. The point of contention? The position of *I'm Alone* at the point of *Wolcott*'s initial interdiction.

Marine practice of the day stated that "the speed of a suspect vessel is a consideration in determining how far out it may be seized." Captain Randall's statement to U.S. authorities made the claim that, when the incident with the U.S. cutter began, *I'm Alone* was anchored "about 15 miles out in safe waters" and not 10.8 as stated by *Wolcott*'s skipper. Further, *I'm Alone*, a mere seven-knot vessel, was at a great disadvantage to the much faster cutter. Plus, Randall added, *I'm Alone*'s engines were in dire need of repair (a fact that couldn't be proven) and consequently, of no help in outrunning *Wolcott*. Randall's claim baffled the Yanks. How was it possible, they asked, for *I'm Alone* to keep a lead on *Wolcott*, the vessel with superior speed? In 1935, the U.S. threw up its hands after rounds of international diplomatic brouhaha and offered compensation to *I'm Alone*'s crew as a settlement of the issue.

EVOLUTION OF RUM-RUNNING VESSELS: 1920–1933

➪ The first vessels were adapted Nova Scotia two- or three-masted fishing schooners called "blacks" by Coast Guard crews, in reference to the darkly painted hulls.

➪ The advent of faster, better-equipped ex-U.S. Navy World War I cutters and destroyers forced rum-runners away from slower schooners to faster and less distinctive crafts.

THE MAKING OF A TRUE RUM-RUNNER

➪ Must-haves: stealth and speed.

➪ Nova Scotia boat builders used a U.S. Navy sub chaser developed near the end of World War I as a model for new rum-runners.

➪ Prized features: small, fast (sixteen-knots flat out), powered by three 660-horsepower gas engines, low-lying, wooden-hulled, cost-effective to build.

➪ The first vessels out of Nova Scotian shipyards were small, under seventy feet and forty gross tons; of sturdy construction, with a flush-decked, low-trim profile; and double-ended. They were mostly diesel-powered coastal freighters with developed transom sterns and grey-painted hulls.

- ➪ By 1928 they were 87 feet and 87 gross tons. By 1932, 98–100 feet and 118 gross tons.
- ➪ Number of rum-runners launched from Metegan: 25
- ➪ Number of rum-runners launched from Shelburne: 22
- ➪ Number of rum-runners launched from Lunenburg and Mahone Bay: 11
- ➪ Number of rum-runners launched from Liverpool: 5
- ➪ Number of rum-runners launched from Dayspring: 3
- ➪ Site of first specific rum-runner launching: Lunenburg
- ➪ Last rum-runner built: *Atacama*
- ➪ Percentage of vessel names beginning with "A" or "M": 23
- ➪ Partial list of rum-runner vessel names:

  Bearcat, Betty and Ida, Cassasa, Consolidated, Gertrude, Jean Grace, Marie, Matilda C., Miserenko, Mudethalapadu, Nan and Edna, Naskwock, Nepsya, Nipigon II, Placentia, Pronto, Semidamus, Teresa Maria.

THE VESSEL HISTORY OF LUNENBURG RUM-RUNNER HUGH CORKUM

1) 3-masted schooner: W. H. Eastwood
2) 125-foot rum-runner disguised as an ocean tug: *Harbour Trader*
3) 80-foot vessel disguised as a side dragger: *Symoy*
4) 100-foot, two-masted fishing schooner: *Kromont*

5) specifically built rum-runners: *Margaret S. II, Alpaca, Pronto, Connisuer, Flora Anne, Frederick H. II*
6) 50-foot decked-over Cape Islander: *Capari*
7) 45-foot Cape Islander: *Herbert P*
8) 60-foot speedboat: *Liberty*
9) 60-foot speedboat: *Marleton*

A general description of a regular motored rum-runner:

➪ Length: 103 feet; breadth: 21 feet; depth: 9 feet 6 inches.

➪ Slim, low (particularly when loaded), single-decked, wooden hull, slight sheer towards the bow, slightly raised wheelhouse forward, small cargo hatch fore and aft, dory stored on very light davits aft.

➪ Powered by Fairbanks-Morse diesel engines.

➪ Cruising speed: 10–12 knots.

➪ Wheelhouse windows fitted with portable steel shutters stowed below when not in use.

➪ Short exhaust pipe protruding above deckhouse.

➪ Short, thin mast with light, sufficient for meeting navigational regulations.

➪ Appearance: easily overlooked, easy to ignore.

➪ Interior: four compartments divided by three bulkheads. Forecastle: space for sleeping, cooking, eating, and recreation, two cargo holds between the engine room. Toilet: a bucket on deck.

➪ Skipper, engineer, and radio operator shared accommodations in the deckhouse.

EVER-FASTER RUM-RUNNERS

➪ U.S.-built speedboats: 60-feet long, mahogany-hulled, bronze shafts, powered by three Liberty airplane engines turning up to 2,100 revs. 20 knots cruising speed, 36 knots "with a bone in her teeth." At full throttle burned a gallon of high-test gas (gas that vaporizes at a lower temperature than regular gas) per minute. Carrying capacity: 250 rum kegs.

Special escape features

➪ Two smokescreen-making capabilities:

1) engineered commercial system consisting of a tank connected with piping to an electronically driven pump, which, in turn, was connected to the engine exhaust manifold tank filled with oil. Suction cock was opened on the tank's bottom, letting oil run to the manifold. Scalding black smoke belched from the exhaust. When the smoke hit the air, it hung low and heavy, virtually impenetrable by sight or searchlight.
2) adding rags, oil, and other noxious items to the main engine exhaust.

CARGO-HANDLING TRICKS

- ➪ To prevent high-powered or machine gun slugs from penetrating through the stern forward to injure or kill the crew, some rum runners installed two bulkheads, six feet high, five inches apart, filling the space in between with ordnance-stopping sand and gravel.
- ➪ At a distribution depot (such as St. Pierre Michelon), wooden liquor crates from overseas were emptied of their contents.
- ➪ Six- or twelve-bottle groups were then packed, padded, and "jacketed" with straw and sewn into canvas bags called "burlaps."
- ➪ Burlaps were easily handled and ideal for quiet transfer at sea from the mother ships to inshore speedboats, with little or no breakage.
- ➪ If the liquor arrived by the can, it was packed by the case—2 two-and-a-half-gallon cans to a case. Otherwise it was shipped by the keg.

Rum-runner Hugh Corkum on transferring kegs at sea:

"The cargo had to be taken out a hatch which was generally my job. I was tall and fairly strong. I had to bend down, grab a keg, lift it over four feet over the hatch covering and throw it onto a rubber tire or mattress to absorb the noise. I could pass them out as fast as they came to me. A full keg weighed about 75

– HUGH CORKUM – RUM RUNNER

pounds, and it was no easy task to lift 300 kegs over the hatch-covering without hitting it and making noise."

ACBN-RADIO: THE AL CAPONE BROADCASTING NETWORK

Trained telegraph operators made up the licensed and unlicensed practitioners during Prohibition.

Unlicensed gangster-controlled radio transmitters were set up to:

- ➪ prearrange rendezvous points for small inshore speedboats and rum fleet ships outside U.S. territorial waters, defined as twelve miles offshore or "an hour's sail from the coastline";
- ➪ order supplies; and
- ➪ conduct internal communications of rum-running organizations, which were generally gangster-managed. Hugh Corkum:

> "The Preventative Service (wireless) operators knew all the rum runner operators by their sending-fist when transmitting. Every "fist" had a different characteristic and could be ID'd. A long message would give them the opportunity to put a fix on our position, and the strength of my signal could give them a fair estimate of the distance between us. So, the trick was to get on and off the air quickly, or, when possible, to stay off the air altogether."

When captured outside Mahone Bay by Coast Guard ship *Laurier* aboard the speedboat *Marleton*, Corkum had to react fast to prevent his radio from being seized.

"I quickly disconnected my transmitter," he said, "and dumped it over the starboard side. I hated to see it go. I also dumped the code book which was a black leather cover book. I had riveted a piece of sheet metal onto the inside front cover so the book would be sure to sink to the bottom immediately."

RUM ROW: "IT BEATS CARRYING SARDINES"

As good an explanation of a Rum Row as you can get, culled from a 1920s Maritime newspaper:

"A Rum Row has been established in the Bay of Fundy. The treaty signed some time ago by the Canadian Government made this bay part

INTERESTING FACTOIDS ABOUT CLANDESTINE RADIO

- handled English and French traffic both in plain text and code.
- sometimes used naval procedure, indicating that some illicit operators were ex-Navy or ex-Coast Guard.
- made up a network of 103 illicit stations between Maine and Florida.
- RCMP eventually intercepted rum-runners' radio signals, cracked encryptions, and laid conspiracy charges leading to convictions by cross-referencing radio instructions with subpoenaed records of banking transactions.

of the high seas. Here the rumrunners may lie at anchor free from the fear of the U.S. prohibition fleet and within a short distance of the Yankee coast. Choice liquors are for sale at a premium price and business is said to be lively, boats of all sorts coming and going in the night. Flashlights and searchlights are plainly visible from the shore."

Tales, lurid and otherwise, were being told of fortunes made overnight by boatmen willing to run a cargo to the American shore. It sure beat carrying sardines.

The attribution and coining of a well-known phrase

- ⇨ The invention of the phrase "Rum Row" was attributed to William S. McCoy, a Jacksonville, Florida, marina and motorboat yard owner who used a fishing schooner as a mother ship just outside the magic three-mile limit to help a confederate with a speedboat smuggle liquor ashore.
- ⇨ McCoy had a reputation for selling only the best booze, thus becoming known as the source of the saying, "the real McCoy."

MORE RUM ROW LORE

- ⇨ Rum Rows were established off the New York, New Jersey, and Maine coastlines (to service the great port cities, New York City and Boston); off Virginia and Delaware; off Florida's Narragansett Bay (where McCoy began his liquor-smuggling enterprise); and off the Texas coast (locale of the *I'm Alone* incident).
- ⇨ Often there were hundreds of mother ships off Rum Row at one time. In one reported incident, there were sixty off the Jersey shore alone.

THE NOVA SCOTIA CONNECTION

- ⇨ Canadian laws prevented liquor consumption except "for medicinal purposes" supported by a note from a doctor, but did not step in to prevent its production and export to the U.S.
- ⇨ The French islands St. Pierre and Michelon, south of Newfoundland and outside the reach of Canadian law enforcement, became a huge offshore base for rum-running to places such as Fire Island, New York.
- ⇨ Gangster Al Capone checked out St. Pierre operations and instructed workers to ship liquor bottles in burlap bags—rather than in the wooden crates they arrived in—to lessen noise.
- ⇨ Wooden crates were used for firewood or building materials. Cutty Sark Villa, fashioned from Cutty Sark crates, still stands on St. Pierre.
- ⇨ Number of gallons of liquor Canada exported to St. Pierre and Michelon in 1929: 747,944
- ⇨ Number of gallons in 1930: 1,624,956
- ⇨ Number of gallons in 1931: 2,042,692

HOW SCARFACE AL'S OUTLAW RADIO TRANSMITTERS ASSISTED NOVA SCOTIA RUM-RUNNERS

Scarface Al Capone, Legs Diamond, and other U.S. gangsters in the booze-smuggling biz liked the big export numbers coming out of St. Pierre and Michelon. As previously mentioned, smugglers had set up operations headquarters in Maine, along with a network of clandestine radio stations dotting the eastern seaboard. Apart from arranging assignations with mother ships, the illicit stations helped locate cruising Coast Guard cutters. The clandestine operators also perpetrated distress hoaxes to distract Coast Guard vessels. Only the most sophisticated wireless systems of the time and the best operators, cryptologists, and code breakers met gangster syndicate favour and employment standards.

AL CAPONE

LIFE AND FAST TIMES FOR THE RUM ROW GUY

- On lawless Rum Row, small-crewed mother ships, sometimes carrying up to two hundred thousand dollars of contraband in a single run, with only themselves to repel attacks, and with no legal recourse, were sitting ducks for pirates.
- Rum runner vessels carried several nameplates that were easily and rapidly switched to confuse the U.S. Coast Guard.
- Big markups, bigger profits—eight dollars at the port of origin sold for sixty dollars on Rum Row.
- Sailors could haul in $100 a month plus a bonus of $150 for every successful trip; a skipper $300 monthly plus a $750 bonus for every trip landed, big money in 1928—more than college-educated engineers pulled down.
- Rum-runners often carried "supercargoes"—agents in charge of the cargo who acted on behalf of the shipper or shipowner.

Hugh Corkum on gangster-syndicate supercargoes, from the book *Both Sides of the Law*:

> "We had an American gangster-style supercargo on board who was in charge of the cargo (12,000 cases of assorted liquors to go to Montaux Point, Long Island from St. Pierre). The captain and the supercargo hated each other and the crew hated both of them. The supercargo wore a 45-calibre revolver in a holster on his belt just like a cowboy. During an onboard drunken spree, the captain told the supercargo, "You son of a bitch, if you want to

start shooting, go ahead, but if you do start, make sure you do a good job, because otherwise you will never live to get a second chance. I will kill you and dump you overboard for shark bait."

One American supercargo was always immaculately groomed and dressed and he always shined and cleaned his binoculars with a one hundred dollar bill, a lot of money in those days.

IN HOT WATERS ON RUM ROW

International law was bent, establishing a twelve-mile limit off U.S. coastlines to "scatter rum runners, lines of floating bars and liquor wholesalers beyond the twelve-mile limit, technically one-hour steaming distance from offshore." But fast U.S. patrol vessels found their new speed and distance rule handicapped them.

In 1925 the U.S. launched the Great Offensive, "a concentrated, determined drive against the rum fleet lying off the coast north of the Delaware Capes."

The offensive, which marshalled all available enforcement vessels in the "Dry Navy," scattered fifty rum-runners back to Canadian ports. ("Dry Navy" was the colloquial term for the U.S. Coast Guard's temperance-enforcement fleet.)

From the Saint John *Telegraph Journal*, May 12, 1925:

> "Glace Bay, Nova Scotia: Two heavily laden liquor craft believed to be a portion of the Atlantic rum fleet unwilling to face the reinforced U.S. Coast Guard's "Dry Navy" have arrived off this port and are offering choice brands of liquors at low prices. Rum, it was reported, was offered at $5.00 a gallon and whisky at $12.00 a case."

- ⇨ Cape Breton rum lovers frequented rum drops at Point Edwards, across the harbour from Sydney.
- ⇨ In July 1928, one rum-runner alone landed 3,500 kegs of rum—200 per night—at Riverport, Dover, Lawrencetown, Northwest Arm, Tor Bay, Sydney, Canso, Pictou, and Shediac.
- ⇨ The "Great Offensive" ended when Dry Navy vessels decamped from the high seas exercise for repairs. In the enforcement void, rum-runners snuck back to Rum Row on moonless, starless nights to resume supplying the demand for booze in the U.S.
- ⇨ Frustrated by the ineffectiveness of trying to bring better-equipped, better-protected, and better-financed smugglers to book, in 1932 federal authorities replaced the feckless Preventative Services of the Customs Department and the ineffective, poorly trained, and under-equipped provincial police forces—staffed largely by political appointment—with the RCMP.
- ⇨ Haplessly, RCMP cutters often remained docked in bad weather. Hugh Corkum explains that rum-runners "generally had better seamanship and speed. Also we stayed at sea regardless of the weather. We really did our best work during stormy weather because we had no fear of Coast Guard and RCMP cutters and the noise from our engines was cut down considerably."

- As so many people were involved in the contraband booze business in and around Lunenburg, the rum-running game was taken none too seriously.
- Legal stalling tactics by top-dollar defence lawyers resulted in adjournments and kept many arrested rum-runners out of jail and back taking care of business on the seas.

RUM ROW SHIVER STORIES AND DIRE HAPPENINGS

- December 1922: a winter storm off Cape Cod shattered three rum-running schooners: *Jennie Bell*, *Madonna V.*, and *Annie L. Spindler.*
- 1931: U.S. authorities gunned down Lunenburg skipper William Cluett, fatally injuring him, during the capture of Nova Scotia rum-runner *Josephine K.* at the mouth of New York Harbour.
- 1933: Canadian agent John "Machine Gun" Kelly killed a sailor when he sprayed bullets at a rum-running vessel unloading booze outside Lunenburg Harbour.
- Prohibition was repealed and officially ended in the U.S. on December 5, 1933.
- Throughout Prohibition's U.S. reign from 1920 to 1933, Nova Scotians were "the principal operators channeling liquor from St. Pierre to the United States."
- Despite Nova Scotia bailing out of "The Noble Experiment" in 1929, the years 1935 to 1936 were rum-running's peak era in the Maritimes, serving "wets" to legislatively "dry" areas.

- In 1938, off Prince Edward Island, schooner *Nellie J. Banks* had the distinction of being the last Atlantic rum-runner captured.
- P.E.I. waved off Prohibition in 1948.

THE BIG QUESTION: WHAT CAME OF ALL OF THIS?

- increased policing
- hiring of temperance inspectors and staff
- increased civil service to handle fines
- expansion of prosecuting and defence attorney services and firms
- government liquor vendors, established by the Liquor Control Acts

A few positive spinoffs:

- Government profits from licensing, smuggling fines and bootlegging fines funded road work, schools, hospitals, pensions, and welfare programs.
- The anti-liquor crusade alerted Nova Scotians to societal problems stemming from alcohol abuse, which in turn led to the creation of Alcoholics Anonymous, Commissions of Alcohol and Drug Dependence, and Mothers Against Drunk Driving.

RUM NOW; RUM FOREVER

Sales of alcoholic beverages in Nova Scotia circa 2004 from Statistics Canada (in units):

- beer: 237,496
- wine: 77,484
- spirits: 161,144

THE VE DAY RIOTS: REVELRY GOES RANCID

It was the perfect storm of conditions for a riot. World War II ended May 5, 1945. By May 7, Halifax's population of 70,000 suddenly ballooned to 130,000 with the addition of navy, army, and merchant servicemen returning from Europe. Overcrowding exacerbated already-inadequate facilities, scarce food (a condition of war rationing), long-standing tensions between military personnel and Halifax residents, poor victory-party planning by the local authorities (closing down restaurants and liquor stores as precautionary measures), and woeful military brass lax in maintaining personnel discipline. No wonder that, with the combustion of spontaneous celebration, the "revelry turned rancid," as a headline in the *Globe and Mail* put it.

The riot timeline for May 7 and 8, 1945

May 7

- Dignitaries' speeches and celebratory fireworks conclude.
- Pent-up emotions in servicemen and civilians boil over.
- A streetcar is set ablaze.
- A mob overturns a police patrol wagon; a sailor ignites its spilled gas.
- A mob "liberates" liquor stores by smashing windows and looting rum, gin, vodka, wines, and beer, turning the VE day revelry into the VE night ructions.
- Eighty-man Halifax police force is virtually powerless to quell the rampage.
- Eventually, rioting peters out as stupors stagger in.

May 8

- Rioting resumes as men, women, and even children storm along Barrington, Hollis, and Granville streets, smashing in windows; looting and torching jewelry outlets, women's wear shops, and drugstores; smashing heads; and, of course, guzzling booze.
- In-use fire hoses are either uncoupled by rioters or, worse, cut.
- Undefended, Keith's Brewery, one of the mob's targets, is spared ruin.
- Order is restored, not by the authorities' intervention, but from utter exhaustion.

Thomas H. Raddall describes the scene in *Halifax, Warden of the North*:

> Bacchanalia followed. Two shops were set afire, and all along the downtown streets sailors, waterfront toughs, and women of all sorts from giddy young girls to wizened hags could be seen smashing bottlenecks on the curbs, drinking themselves senseless, and lolling among the strewn merchandise on the sidewalks and in the gutter. Photographers took pictures. One filthy harridan, staggering along Barrington Street at the height of the riot with her arms full of stolen finery, shrieked again and again, "Never had so much fun in my life."

As for the damage done:

- ➪ 564 businesses damaged
- ➪ 207 shops looted
- ➪ five million dollars property damage, give or take
- ➪ two or three deaths (reports vary)
- ➪ the navy's top officer on the east coast gets fired
- ➪ those crammed in jail faced magistrates who imposed these sentences:

    a) five years for looting
    b) three years for receiving stolen property
    c) two years for vandalism

RUM, IN CONCLUSION

In the 1950s rum slipped a few rungs in popularity after a four-century leading role as first-call in the hearts and minds of imbibing Nova Scotians. All hail the new king, beer.

Once a commodity as hot as an afternoon stroll on planet Mercury, today dethroned King Rum maintains a profile of sorts as a pop-culture icon, in debt to a Nova Scotia-set TV cult comedy, called *Trailer Park Boys*. Julian, actor John Paul Tremblay's character, "never appears without a glass of rum and coke in his hand."

"A drink of inspired blandness," writes Wayne Curtis in "Rum and Coca Cola," published in American Scholar. "Its two main ingredients are both plentiful and cheap. It requires few if any skills to prepare." More exotic and definitely more challenging to prepare are West Indies-inspired concoctions that can be enjoyed in most upscale Nova Scotia cocktail bars—Cuba libres, daiquiris, mai tais, pina coladas, mojitos, and zombies.

For bitterly cold fall and winter nights, can there be anything nicer than a rum toddy (rum, tea or coffee or cocoa, water, and honey, or sugar)? Or a hot buttered rum (light rum, sugar, butter, cloves, and hot water)? And those purist rum stalwarts, Nova Scotia recreational boaters and sailors, hold it to be downright blasphemous, considering Nova Scotia's rich maritime and rum tradition, not to go "sailin' with the captain."

No two ways about it. Rum's story in this province stands as the primary reason Nova Scotia's history pulses, peopled by stirring characters, some as truculent as the times they lived in.

BEER

BACK TO THE BEGINNING

The most pressing question beer drinkers face today is: What goes with beer? The ready answer? More beer. But let's question further. Who invented the beverage in the first place? And how is beer made?

- ➪ Mesopotamians, fiddling about with fermentation, brewed beer sometime circa 4000–3000 BC.
- ➪ Egyptians around 2000 BC produced a "strong and excellent beer" they marketed as Joy Bringer and The Beautiful and Heavenly Making. Making "one of the oldest manufactured forms of nourishment known to civilization" is a pretty straightforward process:

    a) moisten barley (or other grain) until germination
    b) heat to stop germination (this creates malt)
    c) add water and yeast
    d) allow malt sugars to ferment
    e) enjoy the end product—beer

Two factors for creating distinctive flavours

- ➪ a precise recipe
- ➪ brew timing

THE DEVELOPMENT OF INDIA PALE ALE

The Royal Navy, sailing the world in the eighteenth century to maintain and control the British Empire, issued each sailor a ration of one gallon of beer for his own consumption per voyage. A fine source of vitamin D, reasoned the Admiralty. A problem, alas, turned up to curdle their best intentions: beer failed to travel well. During long voyages, often in tropical climes, dismayed tars discovered that their brewskies soured, went flat, and turned punky, so consistently in fact that the navy replaced beer in 1740 with unspoilable rum. From here the beer story develops ashore, on the Indian continent with British imperialists and their business-interest cronies. Glowing reports from agents in the field suggested that India loomed large, tantalizingly so, as a mother lode of wealth. To add weight to British bargaining positions, the Brits stationed a Royal Navy fleet there. Under the fleet's protection, colonists and army units settled in. Now, rum may have met with approval in navy ranks, but not so much with Raj colonials and the army. To beat the heat, one can't beat beer, ran the overriding opinion. But, heat makes it impossible to not only keep beer drinkable, bubbly, and refreshing, but also to produce it. Brewers back home in England attempted to come up with a solution. Many tried but only one succeeded: George Hodgson—a brewer from the Bow Brewery in East London. For forty years, Hodgson had been making ales distinctively lighter in colour than the brown ales, porters, and stouts suds lovers of the times popularized. Hodgson conjured up a new recipe, really a variation on his paler shade of ale. The key to preventing spoilage, he discovered, relied on a higher percentage of alcohol and more hops. His tests proved that his new mix stifled bacteria growth and other nasties that conspired against beer's longevity.

Settling on an appropriate name, Hodgson was delighted when Raj ale lovers partook of Hodgson's India Ale in "staggering" quantities. To compete, other brewers were compelled to come up with their own India Pale Ale versions. When future Nova Scotia brewing kingpin Alexander Keith, as a very young man, entered the brewing world in North England, India Pale Ale was ranked numero uno in the lucrative beer-export market.

THE SURPRISING TALE OF CLAN KEITH'S ORIGINS

- ⇨ Upwardly mobile, a Keith in 1176 was appointed Marischal of Scotland, the official custodian of Royal Regalia and the Protector of the King in Parliament.
- ⇨ The Keith's loyal support of English kings dissolved when Edward I invaded Scotland.
- ⇨ A Keith commanded Robert the Bruce's cavalry at the battle of Bannockburn, ably contributing to a decisive Scottish victory.
- ⇨ A Keith marriage to the daughter of Robert the Bruce's brother-in-law gained the Keith clan impressive and commanding estates in Kincardineshire.
- ⇨ The power of the Keith family expanded until 1715, when the bottom fell out of their fortunes.
- ⇨ Twenty-two-year old George Keith and his brother, James, sided the family with the Jacobite cause against the House of Orange, a miscalculation that stripped the Keiths of all family assets and annual income.
- ⇨ George Keith took flight to Prussia (Germany), where he

became a general in the Prussian army and then Prussian ambassador to Spain.

- ➪ Back in Scotland, several Keiths perished in defence of Scotland against the English at the 1745 Battle of Culloden.
- ➪ 1759 was a happy year for George: a pardon arrived from the King of England.
- ➪ George returned to Scotland and re-purchased some of his lost land (currently, the 13th Earl of Keith calls Keith Hall home in Aberdeenshire).
- ➪ George Keith retired in Prussia and died in 1778.

ALEXANDER KEITH: THE MINI-BIO

- ➪ Seeking fortune and fame as a young Scottish brewmaster with business training, Keith sailed from northern England and arrived in Nova Scotia, catching on as a brewmaster with a local Halifax firm.
- ➪ Three years later, he bought the business. He soon rose to Halifax prominence in:

  a) business
  b) politics
  c) community service

- ➪ Keith was a devoted hubbie (twice) and father (of nine).
- ➪ At the time of his death, he was summed up as "the most hospitable man who ever lived in Halifax."

THE GOOD LIFE A-BREWING

In 1812, James and George's seventeen-year-old nephew, Alexander Keith, set off from the family pile in Scotland to take up an apprenticeship with his uncle, a brewer in Sunderland, northern England. Keith's goal was to glean from his uncle the know-how for making beer and money in the malt business. Beer then (as now) was an essential staple of the diet and culture of the British Isles, and Sunderland supplied much of that staple from its four breweries. In five years, Keith learned the brewing craft and trade. Now twenty-three years old, ambitious, and broke, he headed for Nova Scotia. Numerous Scots, he discovered, had been lured by glowing missives from old pals and relatives newly settled in Nova Scotia. Émigrés took up the Governor of Nova Scotia's land grant offer of two hundred to one thousand acres for their personal usage. Keith joined them, bent on betterment overseas in bonny, boomy New Scotland.

Factors for success in young Keith's favour:

- ⇨ he had a solid general and business education
- ⇨ he had a skilled trade, as he was a certified brewmaster
- ⇨ he experienced no language hurdles
- ⇨ he shared the same Scottish roots as most of the province's citizens
- ⇨ he had an inner core stirred with entrepreneurial fire and resolve

BOUNDING UP FROM BOGGS

Local Halifax merchant and trader Charles Boggs hired Keith as sole brewer and business manager for the oldest brewery in Halifax. Within three years, Keith bought out Boggs and became the brewery's sole proprietor. A steady parade of the thirsty from the navy ranks, naval dockyard, merchant ship crews, and local construction workers rapidly grew Keith's Nova Scotia brewery business. His operation was located on Lower Water Street:

> "Alexander Keith
>
> Begs leave to inform his friends and the public in general, that he has commenced the Brewing Business, in the house lately occupied by Mr. L. Pender, Argyle-street, opposite Dalhousie College, where he intends to Brew Strong Ales, Porter, Ginger Wine, Table and Spruce Beer; and hopes by strict attention to his business, added to his long experience in the above line both in London and Edinburgh, and also in this town, to merit a share of the public patronage and support."

LOVE, MARRIAGE, AND THE HEIRS

Keith married his cousin Eliza Keith on September 30, 1833. They parented nine offspring, but only six lived to adulthood:

1. Eliza Ann (1834–1835).
2. Alexander (1836–1867).
3. Donald George (1838–1886). Never married, no children.
4. Eleanor Jane (1840–1873). Never married, no children.
5. Margaret Louise (1844–1930). Married, two children.
6. Alexandrina Isabella (1846–1897). Married, no children.
7. Marjorie Elizabeth (1848–?). Never married, no children.
8. Ann Emelia (1850–1854).
9. Emma Georgina (1853–1855).

LAYING A CORNERSTONE OF HOPE AND GLORY

On June 17, 1836, a cornerstone was laid for the replacement of the brewery's insufficient wooden structure—a bigger granite building (still standing today). From the *Chronicle Herald*: "The Establishment, when complete, will be first of its kind in British North America; and it is to be hoped Mr. Keith's spirited example will be a stimulus to some of our wealthy citizens to arouse their dormant energies: that they may do good while they have opportunity, laying up in store a good foundation towards the attainment of eternal life."

Report on business at the mid-century mark on Lower Water Street

- ⇨ hogshead (approximately 239 litres) production of porters and ales during the eight "cold" months: 180
- ⇨ hogshead production during the four summer months: 240
- ⇨ annual barley consumption from P.E.I. and the rest of Canada: 15,000 bushels
- ⇨ annual malt consumption from Canada and Scotland: 3,000 bushels
- ⇨ annual hops consumption from Canada, the U.S., and England: 300 bales

ALL ABOARD THE UPWARDLY MOBILE EXPRESS

Keith's business acumen compelled other businessmen to woo him to their boards of directors.

- ⇨ In 1837 Keith joined the board of the Bank of Nova Scotia and Halifax Fire Insurance Company.
- ⇨ 1838 found Keith helping establish the Halifax Marine Insurance Company, whose board he joined.
- ⇨ 1844 found him on the boards of the Colonial Life Assurance Company and the Halifax Gas, Light and Water Company.
- ⇨ In 1856, Keith joined the board of the Halifax Water Company.

A SECRET SOCIETY AND POLITICAL BEDFELLOWS

If secret societies are a whisper, the Masons are a shout. Blame it on their mandate. This oldest and most respected fraternity rallies members to live lives devoted to "high ideals, community service and benevolence." Masons are expected to abide by three fundamental principles, namely:

1) brotherly love, tolerance, respect towards others
2) charity, caring, giving to others, giving through voluntary efforts
3) commitment to truth and high moral standards

At the age of twenty-one, while learning the brewing trade in Sunderland, England, in 1816, Keith joined the Masons. It was a canny move for a young, ambitious businessman. Many top industrialists were members, ideal future contacts for Keith. That the Masons displayed themselves as a non-political organization, welcoming to all religious persuasions, with deeply held concerns for the welfare of orphans, the sick, and the aging, ensured that the contact pool was relatively wide and deep with "good men keen on being better men." Keith fit the ideal, and committed to live his life in accordance with the Masonic code of ethics. In Halifax, he affiliated himself with the Virgin Lodge Number Two and in 1869 he was unanimously elected Grand Master of Masons for Nova Scotia and later elevated to Grand High Priest.

AS A KEITH AND AS A MASON: GOOD WORKS DEPARTMENT

Keith had affiliations with:

- ⇨ The North British Society (to lend helping hands to Scottish émigrés).
- ⇨ The Highland Society of Nova Scotia (to preserve ancient Caledonian culture).
- ⇨ evangelical churches fraught with the belief that "those favoured with privilege and affluence have a Christian obligation to share with the less fortunate, provide assistance to the poor and disadvantaged—especially amongst desperate immigrants."

All this commitment to charitable, fraternal, and cultural organizations meant only one thing: "Tory friends of Alexander Keith persuade a run for public office in the 1840 general election."

Obviously Keith's Masonic obligation to charitable good works and benevolence did not pose a detriment to his selection by a posse of political backroomers representing privilege, power, and prestige.

THE BIG ISSUE IN 1840 POLITICS

Who rules? Should responsible government be in the hands of wealthy members of the community? Or should those "charged with governing be chosen from amongst the majority party in the legislature"?

On the common people's side:

➪ The opposition believed that the House of Assembly should be elected by those (males) from the general populace holding the right to vote.

On the wealth and privilege side:

➪ Legislative Council: the Upper House of the Nova Scotia Legislature based on England's House of Lords, dubbed the Council of 12, consisted of rich, prominent businessmen.

Powers of the 12:

1) arbiters of life and death
2) distributors of patronage
3) members of the court of appeal (judges' decisions could be reviewed or reversed)
4) members of the court of marriage and divorce
5) control of the acts of the Governor General
6) power to introduce legislation
7) right to approve bills passed by House of Assembly before becoming law

Keith's first race (1840):

➪ Reformers won. Keith dusted himself off to try again, this time for a place in civic government. In 1841, he won his race and was elected as councillor for Ward Two.

ALE FELLOW WELL SET

You won't be surprised to learn that, in the 1840s, direct election for the position of mayor didn't exist. City council's executive council, chosen from the rank of its members, wielded the power to appoint the mayor. On October 3, 1843, shortly after the annual September election, Keith's councillor colleagues chose him to serve as mayor. Keith snagged a second term in 1852, but this time by popular vote.

- ⇨ Queen Victoria appointed Keith to membership in the Legislative Council.
- ⇨ The Council of 12, directed by a president acting as chair, picked Keith to be its new president.
- ⇨ Keith served as president from 1867 up to his death in 1873.

Meanwhile, back in the beer business, troubles were fermenting, beginning when Donald G. Keith, Alexander's son, was taken on in the biz as a partner in 1853. The brewery became Alexander Keith and Son Limited.

THE PROBLEM WITH DONALD IS DONALD

Sometimes a son's growth (psychologically and entrepreneurially) is irrevocably stunted when trapped in the shadow cast by a wildly prosperous and celebrated papa. Other times, the requisite dynamic is successfully passed from sire to son or daughter who then, imbued with similar inner drive and purpose, carves out his or her own success. Unfortunately, Alexander's successor-designate, Donald, slotted into the former category. Distrustful by nature, Donald was destined to fail as a businessman. He couldn't focus and lacked interest in the brewing business. Fortunately for the company's well-being, the senior Keith was on hand to keep things on an even keel. But when death claimed him in 1873, Alexander Keith and Sons Limited slipped.

The lacklustre Donald, unmarried and childless, simply couldn't maintain the business's success. At the young age of forty-three, Donald died, leaving the brewery in the hands of his sister, Margaret Louise, and her husband, Doctor William Wickwire, who shed his Kings County medical practice to help run the business.

THE MEASURE OF THE MAN: ALEXANDER KEITH

- ➪ Keith's funeral on December 17, 1873, was believed to be one of the largest of its time ever held in Halifax, a testament to his broad personal popularity and noble Masonic ideals.
- ➪ A large, formidable monument marks Keith's grave in Camp Hill Cemetery.

In a 1915 retrospective, Reverend Allen Pollok, who had known Keith well, described Keith as "the most hospitable man who ever lived in this city, a man of the most generous disposition." Those who knew him, evidently, liked him a lot.

THE WILL AND WHAT HAPPENED AFTERWARD TO ALEXANDER KEITH AND SON LIMITED

First, the will's stipulations:

⇨ the estate of $300,000 (millions by today's standards) was left to his wife, Eliza

⇨ the brewery was to be sold and the proceeds divided into six shares:

a) two shares to Donald
b) one share each to his four surviving daughters

⇨ on Eliza's death, Keith Hall (the family mansion) and its contents were to be sold

ABOUT KEITH HALL

⇨ The hall was designed by Scottish architect David Stirling (also responsible for the Halifax Club and the Art Gallery of Nova Scotia); the building's cornerstone was laid on Hollis Street in 1863.

⇨ Its style: Italianate, with elaborate mouldings, ornately carved marble fireplaces, a facade of honey-coloured Wallace stone accented with carvings and a portico.

⇨ A recessed window over the stairwell radiated the green, gold, red, and blue of the Masonic crest.

- Early into the twentieth century, Keith Hall fell into decline and was taken over for use by the armed forces during World War II.
- In July 1921, Colonel Sidney Oland bought Alexander Keith and Son Limited and Keith Hall, re-purposing the building into the business headquarters of the Oland Brewery Company.

THE OTHER ALEXANDER KEITH

- The number of Alexander Keiths residing in Halifax between 1860 and 1990: around six.

One of these was Alexander Keith, Jr., called Sandy for his red hair. Most definitely not the fabled and honourable brewer as assumed by several historians and writers, Sandy represented the mirror opposite of the Masonic Manifesto held dear by Alexander Keith the brewer. Sandy, the "dynamite fiend," gained notoriety for Civil War profiteering and secret-agenting for the Confederate side, and ultimately, for heinous mass murder. Bad Sandy was the eldest son of John and Christina Keith of Caithness, Scotland, and a nephew of Alexander the brewer with whom he, for a brief period, lived and clerked. Bent on becoming his own man, Bad Sandy left Alexander Keith's home for digs in the Halifax Hotel.

In the years of the American Civil War (1861–1865), Nova Scotia was officially neutral. Still, a good many Nova Scotians sided with President Abraham Lincoln, thanks in no end to New England connections, both familial and entrepreneurial. On the other hand, a fair number of Nova Scotians registered their sympathies with the Southern cause, who sized up far "more civilized and sympathetic to the British Empire." The supply-starved Confederacy dispatched wily agents to Nova Scotia to plead for war support, arguing that the Union Army, should it prevail over the Southern rebels, would then about-face and, by military means, force the "colonies of British North America to join the U.S." Fear choked reason. Citizen groups sprang up as outspoken Confederate supporters. Amongst this lot was Bad Sandy. The Southern agents had a shopping list of needs: foodstuffs, clothing, and weaponry. Sensing a big money-making opportunity in shady war profiteering, Bad Sandy, along with a like-minded group of co-conspirators, enacted enough provocative activities to warrant Halifax being known in some circles as "a centre of treason" and "as secession-minded as Richmond" (Virginia). In one dastardly scheme, Bad Sandy purchased a ship called *Caledonia*. With its cargo hold chock-a-block with matériel, *Caledonia* ran the Northern blockades of Southern ports to make its deliveries. Back in Halifax, police arrested Sandy for being a truculent member of a mob bent on helping a pirate escape justice. Unbelievably, he swindled his blockade-running associates. Because of his unspeakable impertinence, he wisely hightailed it out of Halifax to the United States, where he then parked himself as a model citizen of St. Louis, Missouri. There he married Cecelia Paris and, true to his nature, scammed a substantial fortune from the neighbourhood and prairie folks. One of his outraged victims took it upon himself to hunt down Bad Sandy, hoping to exact revenge and retrieve his money. But Bad Sandy got wind of him, and he and Cecelia made a run for it, to Germany. Flush with ill-gotten cash, Bad Sandy and Cecelia hobnobbed with wealthy Dresden and Leipzig socialites and uppity Saxon

generals. Their fling with the high life was doomed; their money soon dwindled. Desperate for fresh loot, Bad Sandy planned his next big con: blow up passenger ships with dynamite after putting himself in position to collect the insurance payout.

In December 1875 at a port in Bremerhaven, Bad Sandy boarded a passenger ship, *Mosel*, with a bomb stowed in a trunk. He set the timer to allow himself enough time to disembark, but something went horribly amiss and the bomb exploded prematurely. The blast killed eighty and mortally wounded Bad Sandy. Reporters called the incident "the crime of the century." And with that, and the clear up of confusion regarding the two Alexander Keiths, the story of Alexander Keith (the good Keith) ends and the reign of the Olands takes over the narrative of Nova Scotia's brewing royalty.

THE RISE OF THE OLANDS

In 1971, the brewing reign of the Nova Scotia Oland family came to an end when John Labatt Limited bought Oland and Son Limited. The sale ended a stretch of better than one hundred years in the brewing business, a business started not by John James Dunn Oland, but by his English-born wife, Susannah. Long after her death, in 1993, her name was justly inducted into the Nova Scotia Business Hall of Fame. Before we launch into Susannah's remarkable tale in brewing, we'll trace the Oland origins in mini-bio.

THE SCANDINAVIAN CONNECTION

➪ Historians believe the family originated in Oland, a Swedish island or Aland, a Finnish island. The Olands, for certain, eventually turned up in England.

At the point of departure: before the Olands embarked for Nova Scotia

➪ In the 1860s, Halifax, thirty thousand citizens strong, developed into the mercantile centre of the Maritime provinces' universe.

➪ The day's attention-grabbing project: an Intercolonial Railway coupling Pictou and Truro.

➪ John James Dunn Oland and his wife Susannah packed bags and trunks, ready for travel.

➪ They left a Victorian villa near Hampshire for John to work on the railway in thriving New Scotland.

The railway job completed, Oland found himself unemployed. Fortuitously, Oland had a pal, captain of the Royal Artillery Francis DeWinton, aide-de-camp to the governor of Nova Scotia, Sir Fenwick Williams. DeWinton pitched a business suggestion to Oland: Why not market the fabulous homemade beer Susannah had been brewing with three of her sons, John, Conrad, and George, in a shed behind their rented house in Dartmouth? DeWinton cut himself into the plan for $4,800. Completing the backing venture capitalization were George C. Harvey and Thomas Mowbray, both Halifax merchants, who collectively anted up $2,400. The new company's shares split: 1/3 to Oland, 1/3 to DeWinton, 1/3 for Harvey and Mowbray.

THE 1867 PARTNERSHIP AGREEMENT

"The said J. D. Oland shall have the management of the brewery and shall receive as compensation for his services the sum of one cent per gallon of the first one thousand gallons of good saleable ale and porter produced per week and one-half per gallon on the second one thousand gallons produced per week, and one-quarter cent per gallon on all quantities afterward produced per week of a good saleable article, and in addition to such compensation the said J. D. Oland shall be entitled to the free use of the dwelling house attached to the brewery building during the term of this co-partnership, also during such period a sufficient quantity of fuel for use of such dwelling house without charge. He also shall be entitled to keep his three sons employed in such brewery at such wages as shall be agreed upon, provided sufficient work can be found for them."

It was official. The brewing firm of John Oland and Company was up and in business. The date: August 14, 1867.

Oland scouted out an area of twelve-and-a-half acres with a wharf, a spring, and three hundred feet of harbour frontage called Turtle Grove, a.k.a. the Albo Tanyard, and bought the property for the brewery.

THE FIRST OLAND ADVERTISING COPY

▶ found in *McAlpine's City Directory* 1868:

"Turtle Grove Brewery,
Dartmouth
John Oland and Company
Brewers Agents,
Mowbray and Reeves
Head of Hare's Wharf,
Halifax"

SUDDENLY, OUT OF THE BLUE

- In 1870, J. D. Oland, 51, died after being tossed from a horse. After the will probate, George Fraser, formerly of Alexander Keith's Nova Scotia brewery, assumed control along with John C. Oland and Conrad George Oland, with Halifax grocer William Lowe as the fourth Oland partner.
- Fraser changed the brewery name to Fraser, Oland and Company.
- It would be the only time in the brewery's history that any name other than Oland appeared in the company title.

FRASER, OLAND AND COMPANY, 1876

From an ad:

"Constantly on hand, fine, mild and strong ales and extra stout porter in casks and bottles brewed from the famous Turtle Grove Mineral Spring Water. I have examined the sample of water from the Turtle Grove Spring, Dartmouth, and find it nearly pure, containing 3 80/100 grains to the gallon—this consists principally of lime which is a decided advantage in Brewing Malt liquors.

The water after remains in the jar slightly corked for four months, is quite sweet, and free from any decomposition. Our sparkling amber ale is pronounced by competent judges equal in quality to be imported. It has the peculiar flavour and colour of the finest English; Scotch Ales being manufactured from the best Scotch Malt and the finest

Kent Hops. Our Extra Stout Porter is also very fine and specially recommended by Physicians for invalids. We use no Chemicals or Artificial Finings in our Beer the peculiar virtues of the water rendering such ingredients entirely unnecessary."

MORE CHANGES BY FRASER

- ⇨ A tip of his hat to thirsty-throated military patronage—Turtle Grove Brewery became Army and Navy Brewery.
- ⇨ Brewery facilities were upgraded to double hogshead capacity of one hundred per week.
- ⇨ Thanks to Fraser's capital, trade, and technical knowledge, Army and Navy Brewery upped productivity without loss of quality.

ADIEU FRASER; IT'S BEEN SWELL

In 1877 Susannah received an inheritance from her family back in England. She approached Fraser with a buyout offer, which he accepted. Lowe stayed on until 1879, when he opened a wholesale grocery business at the corner of Spring Garden Road and Queen Street in Halifax. With Lowe gone on to other service, Susannah changed the brewery name once more, this time to S. Oland, Sons and Company. The sentiment amongst male-only members of the business community then was: Women have no place in business. End of story. But Susannah had none of that codswallow. Subversively, like female novelists faced with such misogyny, she wisely limited her name to an ambiguous initial. Unobtrusively she took charge of the business, determined "to succeed in a man's world." At her core lay a resolve to call out the prejudices of the day for what they were: misguided and stupid. Wily, razor sharp, and with a prescient judge of business character, she selected son George W. C. Oland's leadership acumen over that of his older brothers, John C. Oland and Conrad G. Oland, as the one to grow the business, writing George in for a two-thirds share in the firm. And, to protect her unmarried daughter, Huldah Sarah, from a spinster's fate, Susannah cut her daughter in for the remaining one-third share. But she needn't have worried on that account—in 1886 Huldah married Halifax photographer Robie Cogswell.

The 1880s brought substantial growth and prosperity for Susannah and her company. Beer and ale, thanks to lower excise duties, scored well because the beverages were cheaper to produce and could be made in greater quantities than liquors and wines.

How good does business get in 1894?

- ⇨ Number of workers employed by the three leading breweries—Keith, Foyle, and Oland: 57
- ⇨ Number of workers employed by Oland in 1894: 30
- ⇨ average annual income in Nova Scotia: $450
- ⇨ average annual income in Ontario: $410

FIVE LOCAL BREWERS FOR OLAND TO CONTEND WITH:

- ▶ Alexander Keith and Son Limited
- ▶ Jas. McLearn
- ▶ P. and J. O'Mullin
- ▶ W. T. Roone and Company
- ▶ Daniel Sullivan

- Rise in value of five existing Nova Scotia breweries between 1881–1891: $194,185 to $200,740.
- Rise in value of four existing Nova Scotia breweries between 1891–1901: from $200,740 to $243,000.

THE TORCH PASSES TO THE SECOND OLAND GENERATION

- On vacation with daughter Huldah in Richmond, Virginia, Susannah Oland suddenly died.
- Halifax newspapers did not report on her amazing career as head of a very successful brewery, referring to her only as "a widow" for fifteen years.

George W. C., the new king of beers, assumed a shaky throne, wobbly because:

- according to the 1890s' Nova Scotia Liquor License Act, breweries needed to obtain licenses in different categories, renewable each year, to have the right to market products.
- Montreal and Toronto business interests, pushing consolidation, hungrily eyeballed Maritime markets.
- 1894's annual expenditures included:

  a) taxes to Dartmouth: $11,500
  b) taxes to the federal government: $15,000
  c) brewer's tax: $100
  d) mallster's tax: $100

Oland's 1893 corporate restructuring

- Partnership downsized to George W. C. Oland and John C. Oland (both brewmasters).
- S. Oland, Sons and Company became a joint stock company: Maritime Brewing and Malting Company Limited.
- John C. became president, and George W. C., vice-president.
- Their big new idea: to corner the suds market as agents for the local Maritime brewing business.

In 1895, the Oland restructuring collapsed:

- A London, Ontario-based syndicate, Halifax Breweries Limited, scooped up the five Maritime breweries.
- It was bye-bye and so long to the Maritime Brewing and Malting Company Limited.
- Halifax Breweries dissolved four out of the five breweries, keeping the former Oland Brewery in operation.
- John C. acted as brewery managing director and, George W. C. acquitted himself ably as brewery manager. Once proprietors, both were now employees.
- Shortly after, George W. C. packed off to P.E.I. to manage Halifax Breweries-owned Brighton Brewery.
- In 1901, John C. shifted gears to take on being a commission agent marketing barley, malt, hops, cork, and brewers' and bottlers' supplies.
- Apart from John C. Oland Jr.'s Cape Breton Brewery (1902–1905), no Oland owned a brewery between 1895 and 1909.

TEMPERANCE REVISITED: BE AFRAID, BE VERY AFRAID

Found in *Health Readers*, a schoolbook published by T. C. Allen Company in 1893. To educate the young against the dire effects of beer consumption on the heart, this warning: "the heart bears this abuse as long as it can and when it stops—the beer drinker is dead."

As we remember from the section on rum, the Canada Temperance Act of 1878 (called the Scott Act after the Honourable Richard M. Scott, the Secretary of State who introduced the bill) found little support (as in, virtually none at all) in the city of Halifax. Halifax stayed wet, thanks in large part to the loyal sudsheads in the army and navy. George W. C. Oland went on the record that the Temperance Act couldn't have helped his brewing business out more. Oland's sold "considerable quantities in Scott Act areas," he said. Then, irony of ironies, a P.E.I. brewery shuttered itself up when beset by temperance activists. Charlottetown's deep thirsts were gratefully slaked by Oland's brews. In 1911, pressure from temperance groups that "nothing short of absolute prohibition would be satisfactory," riled Nova Scotia's Liberal premier, George H. Murray, into pointedly growling, "It was all very well to howl for temperance but one had to make sure what the people wanted. Government [could] not overlook the loss of $20,000–$30,000 annual revenue closing Nova Scotia breweries." Enough said.

A big festering issue of the day: what defined the term "intoxicating liquor"?

- ➩ Alcohol percentage considered too high in Nova Scotia temperance opinion: 2.5 %
- ➩ Alcohol percentage considered well below "intoxicating limit" in the federal government's opinion: 2.5 %
- ➩ Alcohol percentage allowed by 1910 Temperance Act: 3 %
- ➩ A 1911 amendment to the act defined *intoxicating liquors* as "all beverages containing alcohol."
- ➩ These beverages were: rum, brandy, whisky, gin, wine, ale, porter, and lager beer.
- ➩ Specified quantities appointed vendors could sell:

  a) hard liquor —12 ounces
  b) wine—1 quart
  c) beer—1 gallon

There was to be no production of "preparations" containing alcohol not registered under the Patent Medicine Act.

A LITTLE SONG OF WARNING BY MISS CHRISTINE TINLING (TO BE SUNG TO THE TUNE OF "COCKLES AND MUSSELS, ALIVE, ALIVE, OH"):

"I am an abstainer
For sure tis far saner
To leave alone poisons,
whatever their name.
For your stout, beer and
ale, sir,
All all bound to fail, sir.
To do aught of the good
that the brewers would
claim;
REFRAIN:
Drink's hurtful and so
I always say, "No"
For I want to be fully alive,
alive, oh."

BEER

A partial list of preparations not registered under the Proprietary or Patent Medicine Act that could not be legally sold under the Nova Scotia Temperance Act without a prescription:

- ➪ Abolest Invalid Port
- ➪ Bole's Beef, Iron and Wine
- ➪ Centauree Quinina
- ➪ Colsal Tonic Wine
- ➪ Dr. Sproule's Peruvian Tonic
- ➪ Dr. Stanley's Beef, Iron and Wine
- ➪ Elixir Alimentaire
- ➪ Elixir Carlex
- ➪ Elixir d'Étrait de Foie de Morue
- ➪ Elixir Galisaya Compound
- ➪ Elixir of Extract of Cod Liver with Malt
- ➪ Hypophosphates and Wild Cherry
- ➪ Elixir Prolax
- ➪ Ferro Chinato Bucceri
- ➪ Gates Life of Man Bitters (an elixir and a state of mind)
- ➪ Happy Home Tonic Water
- ➪ Hawkins Invalid Port Wine
- ➪ Harvey's Beef, Iron and Wine

ALLOWABLE PURPOSES FOR THE SELLING OF ALCOHOLIC BEVERAGES:

- ▶ mechanical
- ▶ sacramental
- ▶ medicinal
- ▶ manufacturing

- ➪ Harvey's Phosphate Quinine Wine Tonique
- ➪ Harevy's Bon Secours
- ➪ Kennedy's Stomach Bitters
- ➪ Kolatonic
- ➪ Koliiki Troppia
- ➪ Laurentien Glycerphos Compound
- ➪ Le Kina Ferrignieux Durand
- ➪ Le Vin Tonique
- ➪ Madame Vin Tonique
- ➪ Merrills Beef, Iron, Cod Liver Oil Wine
- ➪ Merrills Creme de Menthe Carminative
- ➪ Mustura Tonic
- ➪ O Lux
- ➪ Pepsina Wine
- ➪ Polson's Quinine Tonic Wine
- ➪ Quitvomia
- ➪ Red Heart Tonic Wine
- ➪ Rexall Vegetable Compound
- ➪ Russisches Schlagwasser (yummy)
- ➪ Stello (only to be consumed by starlight)
- ➪ Tonique Digestif et Laxatif St George
- ➪ Turner's Old Tawny Invalid Port Wine
- ➪ Vin Bonaparte (selling this could get the vendor exiled)

- ⇨ Vin Pectoral Guauicole Gentin
- ⇨ Vin Tonique Sans Pariel
- ⇨ Vinotone

On the other hand, it was fine and dandy to sell eau de cologne, bay rum, extracts, tinctures, perfumeries, and methylated spirits.

THE COLD WATER ARMY IN RETREAT

It 1926, the Feds came up with a wonderful and humane idea—an old-age pension plan. The Nova Scotia Tory government of E. N. Rhodes fretted over how best to finance the plan. A Royal Commission's findings, with maybe a trace of irony behind them, recommended that the best funding source for underwriting the pension plan was government sale of liquor. The premier picked himself up off the floor, recovered his equilibrium, and drafted a plebiscite.

The two plebiscite questions of October 1929

1) Are you in favour of continuing the Nova Scotia Temperance Act?
2) Are you in favour of the sale of alcoholic liquors under a Government Control Act?

The plebiscite results

- ⇨ A victory for the government sale of liquor.
- ⇨ On May 1, 1930, the Nova Scotia Liquor Control Commission was established.

- ➪ Number of outlets opened that August: 21
- ➪ Additional outlets opened in September: 6

Sales strategy in a time of temperance

- ➪ Because light wines and beer had lower alcohol percentages, the Nova Scotia Liquor Commission dropped their prices as low as possible to promote their sale.
- ➪ Total sales after first six weeks: $62,587.93
- ➪ Net profit after deducting costs of goods sold, operating costs, and policing: $23,150.82
- ➪ Bottom line: all smiles.

Oland brews carried in government stores

- ➪ Keith's India Pale Ale
- ➪ Keith's Staghead Sparkling Ale
- ➪ Keith's Medicinal Stout
- ➪ Oland's Export Ale
- ➪ Oland's Old Scotia Sparkling Ale
- ➪ Oland's Extra Stout
- ➪ Percentage of sales Keith's and Oland's products accounted for in the Commission's first year of operation: 64 %

Drier days for the cash cow, post-Prohibition

- ➪ Nova Scotia abandoned "The Noble Experiment" (temperance) in 1929

- ➪ In 1930–31, commission sales amounted to $4,958,232.23
- ➪ In 1931–32, sales slumped to $3,767,109.00
- ➪ But—percentage of total sales that were beer and wine: 90 %

THE SON ALSO RISES: MEET COLONEL SIDNEY C. OLAND

The life and times of the Colonel (as he was best known) is the stuff of Masterpiece Theatre presentations. The fascinating story of the larger-than-life character, Sidney Culverwell Oland, rollicks with all of the stuff that Masterpiece Theatre is made of, and more.

The Colonel was born June 17, 1884, the second son of George W. C. and Ella Oland.

- ➪ At fourteen years of age and intrigued by military life, Sid signed on with the 82nd Abegweit Regiment, transferring in 1902 to a light horse regiment in P.E.I.
- ➪ Sidney grew to six feet, four inches tall. A military bearing set off his first commission as provisional lieutenant with the First Halifax Regiment, Canadian Artillery. In 1905, he made lieutenant.

AN INTRIGUING BREAKDOWN OF OLAND'S COSTS

- ▶ manufacturing expenses: 49.91%
- ▶ freight on beer sold: 3.37%
- ▶ excise (federal, provincial, municipal taxes): 27.08%
- ▶ general overhead–trucking, admin: 14.75%
- ▶ Total: 95.11%

Net Profit: 4.89 %

⇨ "We are pleased to report that in 1908, Sidney C. Oland has graduated from the United States Brewers Academy in New York City."

SON RISE IN THE BREWING FIRMAMENT

- ⇨ Sidney took charge of Halifax Breweries, the family's former brewery, which employed his father and brother.
- ⇨ Sidney took a break from the business to advance his soldiering skills at the Royal Canadian Artillery School in Quebec.
- ⇨ In 1909 Sidney purchased Highland Spring Brewery. His delighted father, George W. C., left Halifax Breweries and signed on with Highland Spring as acting president. The Olands were back in the suds game.

COLONEL SIDNEY C. OLAND

THEN SUDDENLY...LOVE

It began benignly enough with a quiet visit paid to his aunt, Sister Baptista, and his sisters at Mount Saint Vincent Academy. Then he saw her: Guillermina Maria del Pilar Socorro Herlinda deBedia y Martel. At first sight of she who will be known as Linda, the love bird sang. She was but seventeen. Happily, for the lovestruck

Sidney, she fancied the tall, handsome young man smitten with her too. Linda's padre, Colonel Antonio deBedia y Labo of Santander, Spain, fought in the Spanish-American War of 1898 in Cuba. When hostilities ended, he settled there, married, and harboured deep animosity towards his enemy in the war, the United States. Scouting out non-American Catholic schools for girls, he found Mount Saint Vincent Academy—the closest in proximity to Cuba. And so, off to the Mount went his daughters. Strict etiquette of the time prevented besotted Sidney and Linda from slipping off alone and when her education wrapped up at the Mount, Linda returned to Cuba. Separations like that can be the kiss of death for romance. Not for Sidney and Linda. Love letters flew back and forth. To see her again, Sidney took a trip to Cuba and not surprisingly, fell in deep like with the city of Havana itself. On a second trip back in March 1911, he and Linda set a wedding date, later tying the nuptual knot on February 13, 1912. Back in Nova Scotia, the couple eased into matrimonial life, taking upscale residency in Halifax's fashionable South End. But the ugly bestirrings in Europe of the war to end all wars ominously threatened to cloud their sunny early days of connubial bliss.

SIDNEY'S WORLD WAR

- June 1914: Sidney received the assignment of preparing the Halifax Harbour defences.
- He took command of the 2nd Divisional Ammunition Column.
- Sidney incorporated his brewing firm and renamed it Oland and Son Limited, with his father, George W. C., as president and himself as vice-president.

- ⇨ Before World War I, during temperance, the biggest market the brewery had was the British West Indies.
- ⇨ In 1910, Oland introduced a non-intoxicating drink, Golden Malt, with an alcohol content of 2%—suds lovers, grimacing, called it "near beer."
- ⇨ The war drew a vast influx of soldiers and sailors into Halifax, the war embarkation point.
- ⇨ 1914 to 1916 were very lucrative years for Oland.
- ⇨ With full Prohibition in force, exports, less than $3,000,000 per annum between 1871 and 1875, swelled to $614,000,000 in the post-war fiscal year ending March 31, 1920.
- ⇨ Called to active duty, Sidney ceded business control to his capable father.
- ⇨ In 1916, the 66th Canadian Field Artillery sprang into existence in Montreal; its commanding officer was Major Sidney C. Oland.
- ⇨ As a member of the Canadian Expeditionary Forces, Sid saw active service in France and Germany.
- ⇨ Linda slipped into England in 1917 to reside in Guilford with four-year-old son Victor deBedia Oland in tow.
- ⇨ On March 18, 1918, twins were born: Amadiat Diana and Bruce Sidney Culverwell.
- ⇨ In June 1919, Major Sidney, demobbed after winning the British War Medal and the Victory Medal, returned with his growing family to Halifax.

While he was overseas, where war was hell, hell also hit Halifax: the Halifax Explosion catastrophe of December 6, 1917. Two ships, the French frigate *Mont Blanc* and the Belgian relief ship *Imo*, collided at the Narrows, a channel between Halifax's inner harbour and the Bedford Basin. For reasons that would never be determined, *Imo* veered into *Mont Blanc*'s path. Ignoring warning whistles, *Imo* held course. *Mont Blanc*, ill-suited for her task—this due to a shortage of more appropriate wartime vessels—carried a volatile cargo of 2,800 tons of explosives: pitric acid (more volatile than TNT), 200 tons of TNT, 35 tons of benzol, and 10 tons of gun cotton. On *Mont Blanc*'s bridge, as horrified Captain Aime LeMeduc watched *Imo*'s bow carve through his ship's hold, freighted with pictric acid, a huge wall of flame whooshed upward. The crew justifiably panicked, and scrambled to abandon ship. Disabled, *Mont Blanc* drifted to Richmond in Halifax's north end. Frantic crews in lifeboats rowed madly for the Dartmouth shore where strollers-by had stopped to watch. Twenty-one agonizing minutes ticked by. Then, the absolutely worst possible outcome of the grim collision. BOOOOOOOOM! The massive explosion killed more than one thousand people in seconds. Another one thousand were horrifically sliced up by shards of flying glass, or grotesquely injured and trapped beneath collapsed debris from shattered buildings. The manifested force was so powerful that *Mont Blanc*'s anchor, the only item left extant of the vessel, was later found by the Northwest Arm, four kilometres away. Insurance appraisers calculated that city property losses totalled in the sixteen- to seventeen-million-dollar range. Donations soon arrived. The Halifax Relief Commission handed out five million dollars to the needy and wounded. Acting chief engineer for Halifax, H. W. Johnston, told officials that flattened Halifax must "replan and rebuild in accordance with modern ideas of city planning." Namely, a "series of boulevards lined with row houses built of a newly developed fire preventative material called hydrostone."

HOW THE OLANDS FARED

- Halifax Breweries was flattened along with Oland Brewery in the north end.
- Working for Halifax Breweries, Conrad George Oland, 67, who fifty years earlier had helped his mother Susannah and his two brothers brew and bottle her beer recipe, died in the blast.
- Total financial loss to Oland and Son Limited: $87,922
- Insurance settlement settled in 1919: $50,000
- Sidney pondered the feasibility of rebuilding in the face of prohibition.
- In 1918 George W. C. Oland, owner of New Brunswick's Simeon Jones Red Ball Brewery, wrangled a city permit to throw up a one-storey, seventy-five-foot-long pitched roof shed for use as a mineral water manufacturing plant.

AFTER THE WAR WAS OVER

- Ever the military man, Sidney attached himself to the Canadian Army Militia in 1920, retiring in 1922 as Lieutenant Colonel. Henceforth, until his death fifty-five years later, he would be referred to as Colonel Oland, and enjoy appointments as aide-de-camp to not one but three Governors General of Canada: the Earl of Bessborough, Lord Tweedsmuir, and the Earl of Athlone.
- With the family in Cuba in 1922, his fourth child, Don Jaime, was born (throughout his life, mildly miffing him, Nova Scotians assume Don Oland's thoroughly Spanish name is a derivative of Donald).

- ⇨ While in Cuba, Sidney firmed up Havana as a hot market for Oland's New Brunswick beer.
- ⇨ Then he managed to shore up the same market in Jamaica.

THE COLONEL'S CONUNDRUM

Post-explosion, the Halifax business community reeled from the effects of the horrific blast, a post-war recession, low population growth, an outflow of Maritimers from the region, adverse tariff barriers and freight rates imposed by the feds, the absence of a substantial urban industrial centre with which to compete industrially and commercially with the rest of Canada, and an impotent assertion of interests on the national stage. Plus, there was that lingering brewing bugaboo, Prohibition.

Halifax didn't look like a smart choice for rebuilding in Sidney's estimation. He entertained other sites. He was known in Cuba, and his wife was Cuban, with family connections that stretched all the way back to Spain. So, you might think they went off to Cuba. But you'd be wrong. Try California. It seems Colonel Sid harboured a deep-rooted interest in the movies. Keen to try his luck in the film world, Colonel Sid packed bags and trunks and, just like that, whisked the family off to Tinseltown.

HOORAY FOR HOLLYWOOD

At first Sidney and the family stayed in a house rented by his parents in Hollywood. Then they moved into a domicile of their own. The socialization was fabulous. The Olands hobnobbed with actors, big-time stars like Lillian Gish, the acerbically witty Tallulah Bankhead, and the petite dynamo from Toronto, Mary Pickford. Walter Oland, a distant cousin and popular actor (who gained fame and success as Charlie Chan in the flicks), inspired Sidney to try his luck on the silver screen. As a bona fide military man, he was cast in a bit role, ironically in *All Quiet On The Western Front*—a film portraying the war from the German point of view. Sidney was not much of a thespian, but savvy movie producers sought him out as a film advisor on British and Canadian military dress, decorations, and protocol. Meanwhile, back in Halifax, problems in the shattered business forced Oland and Son to declare bankruptcy. It wouldn't last long. Sidney and family bade farewell to Hollywood and in 1925 resettled in Halifax.

BACK TO (AND IN) BUSINESS ONE MORE TIME

- ➪ The family installed in a house on Birmingham Street, and Sid set himself up to surf the crest of a freshening wave of economic improvement.
- ➪ In June 1925, the Registry of Joint Stock Company gave thumbs-up to the reinstatement of Oland and Son as a company under the Nova Scotia Companies Act, meaning Sid had decided to rebuild the brewery rather than relocate elsewhere.

- Sid avoided bank loans by securing a thirty-five-thousand dollar mortgage from his supportive father, George W. C., to buddy-up with the Halifax Relief Commission's Halifax Explosion settlement of fifty thousand dollars of rebuilding capital.
- The new brewery, designed by architect William M. Brown, would be a two-storey brick structure marked by a stylish Greek Revival-style entrance and be sited to front onto Agricola Street, then one of the busiest commercial streets in the city.

REASONS FOR OPTIMISM IN 1925–26

- After sixteen years it had become obvious even to the most strident abolitionist that prohibition was wheezing its last dry-mouth breaths.
- There was a marked increase in "illicit trafficking," pure hell to detect and to snuff out by control officials and authorities.
- Thanks to its elevated alcohol content, chief temperance target rum allowed beer consumption, slipping quietly past watchdogs between 1926 and 1929, to climb substantially.
- Beer sales, unlike ardent spirits, were legally made to government vendors and to export markets.
- 1925 tourism rose past the one million visitor mark, placing Nova Scotia as the third-most-popular tourist province, after Ontario and P.E.I.
- The feds gave one million dollars to Halifax for construction of new grain elevators and a Canadian National Railroad terminal near Point Pleasant Park on the harbourfront.

THE COLONEL CAPTURES A CASTLE

- ➪ In 1927 Sidney bought a house of "grand proportions" occupying "extensive grounds on Young Avenue"—a street apportioned to "accommodate stylish homes of the affluent."
- ➪ The house, which would be known as Oland's Castle or Lindola (a blending of Linda and Oland)—had been a 1901 commission for the architecture firm Hopson Brothers from Alexander Hobrecker, a Halifax merchant.
- ➪ Hobrecker, of German extraction, wanted a house reminiscent of his family's castle in Germany.
- ➪ A rumour floated around that Hobrecker intended to offer the house as home base and headquarters for the Kaiser should he flee Germany to Canada.
- ➪ The house was constructed entirely of marble culled from Marble Mountain, Cape Breton.

THE BIG GULP AND LONG SWALLOW OF 1928

- ➪ Charlotte Wickwire, one of Alexander Keith's three daughters, put Nova Scotia's primary brewery, Alexander Keith and Son Limited, up for sale.
- ➪ Sid had a look over the enterprise, noting that, as one of Halifax's leading businesses, Alexander Keith and Son Limited boasted an excellent credit rating and impressive property value.

- ⇨ Sidney consulted his father with an eye to purchasing the firm: George W. C. gave his blessing.
- ⇨ Sidney snapped up Keith and with that, Oland and Son Limited became the monopolistic Monarch of Ales and Suds.
- ⇨ When George W. C. passed away January 25, 1933, Sid assumed the role of president of Oland and Son Limited.

WORLD WAR TWO DAZE IN NOVA SCOTIA: 1939–1945

Prohibition had been dead for ten years in 1939. So you'd think government regulators would have kicked back, poured themselves a drink, and asked themselves, "What were we thinking?"

You'd think. But nope. Liquor laws remained strict. And rigid. In Halifax, for example, it was impossible to find a licensed dining room, a bar, or even a single local in town. They were as rare as step-dancing fish.

TAXES OF THE TIMES

- ▶ Feds: income tax, excess profits' tax, brewer's licence tax, malt excise tax, sales tax on imports of raw materials, duty and excise tax on imports, excise stamp tax.
- ▶ Nova Scotia: income tax on capital by place of business, brewer's licence, warehouse licence, sales tax, auto and truck licence, gas tax.
- ▶ Municipality: property tax and business tax.

The insular small town of Halifax changed when armed forces personnel and their families streamed into the city, which was serving as the east coast send-off port for the war in Europe. Lodging was at a premium. Hotel lounges became dormitories. Rent gouging broke out. Some armed forces personnel shelled out cash for half of a double bed. As for entertainment outlets to distract newcomers from dismal digs and cramped conditions, there were only two movie theatres and a bevy of rentable babes to shoulder the escapist burden. Military canteens offered hard stuff for officers, beer for the boys.

Beer sales rose 91 %, meaning increased revenue for Oland's.

- 1939: $217,000
- 1940: $414,050
- revenue increase to Nova Scotia Liquor Commission from beer tax: 81.4 %

At Oland's, Colonel Sid handled the business with grand-nephew and brewmaster David Falconer. Sid's three sons, Bruce Sidney Culverwell, Don Jaime, and Victor deBelia, joined the forces to participate in the war effort. The war years in Halifax saw increased employment (80 % of the brewery's workforce were women), higher wages, and upsurges in sales of distilled spirits and beer, no doubt a result of the swell in population. Despite some troubling living conditions, the city brain trust continued to cling to lack of wisdom and insight as bulwarks of propriety against plebian enjoyment of alcoholic beverages. When the May 5, 1945, VE day riots (the second Halifax Explosion) erupted, Colonel Sidney reacted by hurrying to the Keith's Brewery warehouse, throwing open the doors and personally passing out cartons of beer to rampaging service personnel and civilians. For that wise move, the brewery remained intact. Never has so much been saved from so many by so few. For the cool-headed Colonel, it was his finest hour.

SOME LIQUOR LAW CANS AND CAN'TS:

1) No drinking outdoors.
2) Sharing a bottle, no way.
3) Carrying an opened bottle—prohibited.
4) Open a bottle, and the contents must be immediately consumed.
5) The only legal drinking establishment: your home (drink 'em if ya've got one—a home, that is).
6) The Nova Scotia Liquor Commission kept standard business hours: closed Saturdays.

THE POST-WAR YEARS

Oland and Son Limited's head office switched from Agricola Street to Keith Hall on Hollis Street when the firm became a publicly owned company.

In 1947:

⇨ new foreign exchange regulations flattened reliable markets in the West Indies.

- ➪ percentage drop in Nova Scotia Liquor Commission beer sales: 11 %
- ➪ nonetheless, Oland's expanded its business as, in 1948, the slide in beer sales stopped and took a welcome upturn.
- ➪ Oland's secured its status as sole supplier of draught beer to Nova Scotia taverns.
- ➪ company earnings were up from $56,975.60 to $238,342.14

BEER

In 1948:

- ➪ Oland and Son Quebec Limited was established, licensed to sell suds throughout La Belle Province.

Oland and Son Limited entered the ale competition in both the prestigious Brussels and London International Brewers Trade Fairs. L'Institut International d'Alimentation, tasters of discerning palates, deemed Oland's ales to be major-prize worthy. The Brits bestowed upon Oland's the Star of Excellence in London and first prize in ales at the British Brewers' Exhibition. Back home in Nova Scotia, a change in federal government policy awarded an allowance of larger beer exports to some West Indies agents. When you're hot, you're hot.

Colonel Sid controlled three of the four Maritime breweries in 1958 when he bought Red Ball Brewery in New Brunswick and changed its name to Oland's Brewery Limited.

But in the 1950s, however:

- ➪ beer consumption peaked
- ➪ beer consumption increased less than 5 % per capita
- ➪ beer continued to outstrip wine and spirits in sales

And in 1953–1959:

- ➪ beer sales: $1,534,000
- ➪ spirits sales: $850,000
- ➪ wine sales: $98,000

In 1958 Nova Scotia suds consumption slumped to below the national average (yikes).

- ➪ percentage rise in wine consumption: 66 %
- ➪ percentage rise in spirits consumption: 21 %
- ➪ percentage rise in beer consumption: 2 %

HEY! WHAT'S GOING ON HERE?

Pricing. That what was at the crux of the suds problem. Fault didn't lie with the brewers but with the Nova Scotia Liquor Commission. The NSLC marked up beer prices thusly:

a) for large (quart) bottles of beer: 28 %
b) for small (pint) bottles of beer: 47 %

In contrast, the NSLC only marked up:

c) hard liquor and whisky 15 %
d) rum 6 %
e) domestic wine 4 %

But, foreign wine prices were lowered.

OLAND'S IN THE SWINGIN' '60S:

Oland's focus: expansion and modernization. And withstanding a withering challenge to Oland's supremacy in suds and ales from, of all people, Colonel Sidney's older bro, George Bauld Oland.

James Ready Brewery, renamed New Brunswick Brewery, had been managed by George Bauld from the time of its purchase by Colonel Sidney and George's father, George W. C. New Brunswick Brewery dominated the New Brunswick beer market. And then came another name change, this time to one very recognizable today in Nova Scotia: Moosehead Brewery. When Moosehead Brewery went up in a newly inaugurated

MORE PROVINCIAL GOVERNMENT DIRECTIVES:

- Liquor could not be sold by the glass.
- Hotels and restaurants, not "generally licensed," were permitted to serve liquor solely with meals.
- It was verboten for unescorted women to imbibe in lounges or taverns. The only exception: clubs.
- Maximum allowed beer alcohol content: 4.4 % (for light beer: 2 %).
- In 1959 only thirteen licensed dining rooms existed, and of thirty-eight taverns, six were in Halifax.
- There was 1 outlet per 13,000 guzzlers of drinking age in Nova Scotia in compared to the national average of 1 per 2,500.
- All in all, the measures were a clumsy, stumbling, and foul-smelling downer for the Nova Scotia tourist industry.

Halifax industrial park, Burnside, competition for Oland loomed large. Moosehead itched to take on Oland's monolopy. The parvenu brewery represented for the first time in close to sixty years a brewing enterprise not controlled by either Colonel Sid or any of his three sons. How did the upstart fare?

- ⇨ In 1964 Oland's sales plunged 30 %
- ⇨ In 1965 Oland's sales plummeted a further 45 %

Oland's woes weren't limited to Moosehead's competition. Taxes and tight government restrictions on advertising also had the effect of diluting Oland's entrepreneurial zazz. Under onerous federal radio and TV advertising restrictions, broadcasting advertising was as easy as swimming to the moon. The rules permitted companies to unobtrusively slip in their firm's name only as a sponsor. Brand advertising was absolutely forbidden.

THE BLUENOSE SOLUTION

In 1955, the Oland brewery created Schooner Beer. The brand's target market: New England—in particular, Boston. Schooner Beer did breakaway business in Massachusetts and proved to be a gullet-fave with Nova Scotia beer drinkers as well. The brand spawned a boffo idea for "brand promotion in spectacular fashion." What better way to shill Oland suds on a national, even international, level than by putting a replica (call it...*Bluenose II*) of the famed and iconic schooner on the flip side of the dime.

The "sight of a traditional schooner, her sails billowing, visiting coastal towns and villages in the Atlantic Provinces with a hold filled with beer, has to be expected to gladden many a Maritime heart." Colonel Sidney loved the idea. He hired naval architect and original designer of *Bluenose*, William Roue, shipbuilder John Rhueland, and *Bluenose*'s fabled captain, Angus Walters. In February 1963 Colonel Sid was in Lunenburg at Smith and Rhueland for the ceremonial laying of the keel. Both he and an honorary captain, Angus Walters, pounded a golden spike into the ship's keel as the new captain, Ellsworth Coggins, a master mariner and former captain of the movie ship *Bounty* looked on. As the shipbuilding proceeded, tangible differences from *Bluenose I* took shape. *Bluenose II* featured:

- five staterooms;
- a captain's cabin;
- a chartroom aft;
- the engine forward;
- crew's quarters in the forecastle, including staterooms for the mate and engineer

⇨ modern equipment, such as a ship-to-shore radio telephone, direction finder, fathometer, internal communications system, and a combined heating and air-conditioning system.

Wednesday July 24, 1963. A crowd of fifteen thousand looked on with barely suppressed smiles as Linda Oland cracked a bottle of champers across *Bluenose II*'s spanking new bow. Shortly after, it was down the slip with her, into Lunenburg Harbour. William Roue, the vessel's architect, wanted to race it. The Colonel wanted the ship to promote Oland beer. While these "wants" competed, a son of Amadita (née Oland) and Norman Stanbury, folksinger Michael Stanbury, soothed souls as he and his folk group, The Townsmen, warbled "The Ballad of the Bluenose," a musical selection he penned for the occasion. Meanwhile, Oland's head office pulled off a propitious promotional (albeit less prosaic) tie-in with the vessel—appropriately, a beer label. In 1965, export brand Schooner Beer and export-only Schooner Ale were emblazoned with an etching of *Bluenose* laid over a map of the Maritime provinces. In the end, *Bluenose II* neither raced nor freighted Schooner Beer for short runs to coastal towns. Instead, the schooner shifted purpose, assuming celebrity status as Official Host Ship (and public attraction) at Expo '67, Montreal's fabulous World's Fair. Four years later, Oland and Son Limited divested themselves of *Bluenose II*, selling it to the Nova Scotia government for a dollar. The price of storied glory was the price of promo folly. Not that you'd notice though. Broader and better advertising avenues opened for Oland's. The company sponsored TV shows: *Ripcord, Man and the Challenge, The Dick Powell Show*, and four TV specials featuring the Scott Singers of Cape Breton. Baseball, hockey, and soccer also thrived with Oland sponsorship support.

ENDGAME

- In 1966, at the age of 74, Linda Oland died.
- Victor deBedia Oland tendered his resignation as the breweries' president in 1968 to take up a new posting as the twenty-fourth lieutenant-governor of Nova Scotia.
- In 1969, Colonel Sidney relinquished presidency of Oland and Son Limited in favour of the final Oland president of the firm, Bruce S. C.
- Bruce S. C. had become a Royal Canadian Navy Commodore with HMCS *Scotian* back in 1951.

LATE 1960S AND EARLY 1970S

- Ontario brewing juggernaut John Labatt Limited, having stomped successfully into the New Brunswick and Newfoundland markets, scoped out Nova Scotia.
- Labatt offered to buy Oland and Son Limited and the offer was accepted in 1971.

The Reasons:

- new business models (going big and national as powerful oligarchial conglomerates) spelled doom for parochial businesses;
- business survival warranted nationwide product marketing; and
- rising production costs limited competitive pricing flexibility.

Under Labatt's control:

- ⇨ Oland and Son Limited morphed into Oland Breweries Limited;
- ⇨ Bruce S. C. stayed on as president, as did the staff;
- ⇨ previously planned expansion continued unabated;
- ⇨ the great Oland brewing tradition begun by Susannah's home-brew and John James Dunn Oland's business wits in 1867 in Dartmouth, came to its end.

EPILOGUE

The last of the old-time Maritime beer barons, Colonel Sid, lived out his final days in Lindola, dying at the ripe old age of 91 on November 17, 1977.

BREW'S WHO 2: THE RISE OF CRAFT BREWERIES AND BREW PUBS

From *Fermenting Revolution: How to Drink Beer and Save the World* **by Chris O'Brien:**

"Could beer save the world? In the age of globalization, we are capable of the wholesale destruction of life on the Earth, not to mention the elimination of unique beer cultures around the world. We are in grave need of some life-affirming energy to counterbalance this penchant for mass annihilation. Beer can provide some of the answers. The craft beer movement is putting into practice a sustainability model called "bioregionalism." Brewers are using small-scale technologies, developing local markets, reducing packaging and shipping, making use of locally available materials and reducing overall waste through eco-industrial design. Small local breweries and brewer pubs are innovating closed-loop systems that move away from wasteful, polluting oil-dependent business practices."

Nova Scotia can brag of several fine craft breweries and brew pubs, each doing its bit for world suds diversity and long-term eco-sustainability. Okay, it's a fair assumption that their formations speak more to a passion for producing varieties of flavourful beers distinct from the corporate ales manufactured by the all-powerful mega-merger brew boys than to planetary concerns. But what the heck. It's a win-win outcome. Here, now, is a look at some of the bright stars in Nova Scotia's craft beer firmament.

GARRISON BREWING COMPANY

Garrison's president, Brian Titus, a former naval diving officer, is often considered responsible for "introducing the craft beer movement to Nova Scotians." For beer drinkers who gravitate towards unique and singular tastes, Garrison, since its establishment in 1997, has offered these distinctive brews:

- Raspberry Wheat Ale
- Tall Ship Amber
- Irish Red Ale (Garrison's first product)
- Nut Brown
- Martello Stout
- Jalapeno Ale
- Khybeer Moka Ale

▶ derivation for the word 'beer': from the Latin verb *bibre* meaning "to drink"

Khybeer Moka Ale

"Created in conjunction with the Khyber Club, the hangout for students at NSCAD (Nova Scotia College of Art and Design), Khybeer Moka Ale has graduated into its own special niche. Flavourful nut brown ale and fresh, locally roasted Java Blend Espresso, combine to deliver an exceptional taste experience. Just like good art, Khybeer challenges the senses and satisfies your soul."

Jalapeno Ale

"Unique in the Maritimes (and anywhere north of Santa Fe), our Jalapeno Ale will cool you down and warm you up

all at the same time. Our refreshing Tall Ship Amber Ale is loaded with Jalapeno, Habanero, Scotch Bonnet and Jamaican Hot Peppers to create a truly unusual brew. This beer is great for lovers of all things spicy and hot, and a killer secret weapon in the kitchen and on the grill."

Note usage of words that cannily define craft breweries and brew pubs displayed in these adver-factoids:

1) "created in conjunction with..."
2) "its own special niche..."
3) "deliver an exceptional taste experience..."
4) "unique in the Maritimes..."
5) "to create a truly unusual brew..."

BEER

Unlike corporate brews (no surprises), craft beers can elicit strong opinions and wide-ranging reactions.

A sample of comments culled from beer blogs:

- ⇨ "I must say I had the Jalapeno and am not a fan. I say this of any hot pepper beer. A trick that I do not see the need of."
- ⇨ "Dude, while I was drinking a Garrison Raspberry Wheat in downtown Halifax, I was somehow drawn by the powers that be to your beer blog. I love it. I'm an Ontario native, but have been in Halifax for 2 years. This beer rocks."

FIFTEEN SHORT BEERS ABOUT THE GARRISON BREWING COMPANY

1) Garrison founder Brian Titus, fact-finding with the intention of establishing a craft brewery, checked out Newfoundland and British Columbia microbreweries.

   "People," Titus was quoted as saying, "felt comfortable sharing their knowledge with me and it was time well-spent. There's a lot of camaraderie in the industry, and I was able to gain valuable insight."

2) Persistence and enthusiasm combined to draw in investors to provide venture capital for buying expensive equipment for brewing darker ales by traditional methods.

3) Design and fabrication of tanks and other integral equipment for the brewing process were handled by Diversified Metals Engineering of Charlottetown, P.E.I.

4) The brewhouse is made up of a single-step infusion mash tun (a large tank), a propane-fired kettle, and a whirlpool.

5) The process:

- Two days of brewing to fill each fermenter, outputting 60–75 large kegs of product.
- Over a span of fourteen days, unfermented beer (the wort) is fermented warm, conditioned cold, naturally carbonated, and filtered.
- The pure draught beer and ales—unpasteurized, devoid of enhancers or preservatives—are bottled or kegged.

6) Ingredients

1) Canadian and imported roast barley malts;
2) Washington's Yakima Valley aromatic hops;
3) double-filtered water; and
4) hearty and robust ale yeast.

7) Super-smart packaging, namely twenty-litre kegs for squeezing into tight places in bars, found room amidst the Big Brew Boys to sell product in "hot drinking spots."

8) Growth after one year in business: 50 %

9) Annual growth percentage since: 5–6 %

10) Garrison moved to a snazzy new brewery complex at Pier 21 in Halifax.

11) Garrison capacity: 350,000 to 500,000 bottles of draught ales and specialty brews per year.

12) The name "Garrison" honours Halifax's early status as a garrison town.

13) The first garrison town brewer was William Steel, who in 1754 quenched the thirsts of early settlers and troops amassed on Citadel Hill.

14) Garrison's niche marketing: the sponsorship of the Atlantic Jazz Festival and the Atlantic Film Festival.

"Those events," Titus was reported as saying, "fit our profile well. We sponsor sports too, but in our case, we work with squash tournaments rather than hockey or football."

15) For Garrison-fuelled partying, beverages are offered in:

1) single bottles;
2) six-pack party mixes;
3) 19.5-litre kegs (56 twelve-ounce glasses of brew);
4) 50-litre kegs (145 twelve-ounce glasses of brew); and
5) growlers (glass jugs holding approximately six bottles).

PROPELLER BREWING COMPANY

The man behind Propeller, a film-industry prop master named John Allen, began his brewing career filling in slack times between film and TV productions with homebrewing. After quaffing his beers and ales, Allen's friends and colleagues professed their abiding love for his brews, so much so that in 1997, Allen became a brewer. Steadier than film and TV work, that's for sure. With the help of pals and family, Allen proclaimed himself a brewmaster for good, and opened Propeller Brewing Company.

The thought processes behind the company name:

1) A facile transformation from props to propeller.
2) It's "a playful celebration of Nova Scotia's rich seafaring tradition while avoiding the over-worked symbols from the golden age of sail."
3) Propeller is as uniquely Nova Scotian as John Patch of Yarmouth, Nova Scotia, inventor of the propeller in the 1830s. (Corrupt American patent granters swindled Patch out of a patent for the propeller, and he died a pauper.)

Allen received sage brewing advice and know-how from James Pryor, a greybeard of the British beer business with experience from such companies as Courage, Bass, and Whitbread.

The list of Propeller ingredients

- ⇨ clean-filtered water
- ⇨ malted barley from Saskatchewan mixed with judiciously chosen specialty malts from producers over the pond in Europe and Great Britain.

Propeller's brewing process:

a) Malt milled by Propeller is combined with heated water, which creates mash.
b) The sweet extract is collected in kettles and brought to a boil.
c) Whole leaf hops are added to "impart flavour and to act as natural preservative."
d) This liquid mix (the wort) cools.
e) A special yeast culture (kept and maintained at Dalhousie University) is stirred in.

f) Fermentation takes place.
g) After the yeast does its yeasty thing, the brewmaster tweaks the product for proper colour and clarity.
h) The temperature is lowered for a week to condition the brew.
i) The beer is filtered.
j) It is then bottled or keg-filled, unpasteurized and without preservatives.

PROPELLER'S SPECIALTY ACTS AND PARTY PIECES

- Propeller Honey Wheat
- Propeller Seasonal Ales
- Propeller I.P.A. (a linen-lifter with a 6.5 % alcohol content)
- Propeller Pumpkin Ale
- Spiced Christmas Ale
- Propeller Revolution
- Imperial Russian Stout

No brash claim this, in the words of BJCP beer judge Jeff Pinkey, Propellor is "Very refreshing, well-balanced and holding great promise as a true session beer. Reminiscent of Fuller's London Pride. Very good beer." (BJCP, mainly a North American organization, is an initialism for Beer Judge Certification Program. The program aims "to promote beer literacy and appreciation of real beer and to recognize beer tasting and evaluation skills.")

⇨ More substantiation: from beverage writer Sean Wood, found in the Halifax *Chronicle-Herald*: "Propeller's London Porter is perhaps the best locally brewed beer I have ever tasted."

⇨ If that weren't all: Propeller Extra Special Bitter cops a Gold Medal at the 2006 World Beer Championship (bitter is traditionally a draught ale pulled fresh under no pressure at cellar temperatures by a gravity or hand-pump dispenser—now you know).

BEER

A BEER AND BEER LITERACY LIST FOR PROPELLER AFICIONADOS

- Propeller Pale Ale: modeled after classic British pale ales; golden to even copper-coloured, dry, with a very definite hop taste; brewed to differentiate from the darker London Porter.
- Propeller London Porter: patterned after a strong, nourishing beverage for the labouring classes (such as porters).

ONE SMALL SWALLOWED

Maritime Beer Company of Dartmouth, Nova Scotia, like microbreweries Garrison and Propeller, sprang up in 1997 and captured four percent of the Atlantic market with these colourfully monikered brands:

1) Atlantic Storm
2) I.P.A. (India Pale Ale)
3) Privateers Classic Ale
4) Halifax 1749 Stone Fired Ale
5) Kings Honey Amber Ale
6) Frosted Frog (imagine the hops to produce this brew)
7) Black Pearl Cream Ale

In 2000, Sleeman Brewing and Malting Company Limited of Guelph, Ontario, took over Maritime Beer Company.

MUGSHOTS

- Kevin Keefe, who many involved in the field cite as the godfather of the brew pub concept in Canada, established the most excellent Granite Brewery and Brewpub in Halifax, lauded for its Best Bitter, Best Bitter Special (dry hopped), Peculiar, and Keefe's Irish Stout.
- John Shippey's Brewpub threw open its doors on Privateers Wharf in Halifax in 2000 to serve its six to eight handcrafted lagers and ales on tap to Haligonians, delighted tourists, and university students.

⇨ Rogue's Roost Ale House in Halifax, a going concern since 1998, brews five steam-fired beers, which include a German-style wheat beer with the aroma of bananas, citrus, and cloves, as well as the light-bodied, smooth-textured fan favourite, Rogue's Amber.

⇨ Wolfville's beer lovers enjoy the ales and lagers found in Paddy's Brewpub and Rosie's Restaurant, founded in 1992.

⇨ Paddy's Pub and Rosie's Restaurant in Kentville makes Annapolis Valley Ale, Raven Ale, Acadian Cream Ale, Gaspereau Pilsner, and Chimney Swift Stout for its lucky customers.

➪ Guysborough's pub devotees are well served by the Rare Bird Pub and Chedabucto Bay Brewing Company.

➪ The Queen Molly, established in 1997, aims to satisfy beer lovers in Yarmouth.

Can beer save the world? If beer can help, stellar distinctive brews from Nova Scotia's corps of fine craft breweries and brew pubs are effecting a tasty start in the right direction.

MISCELLANY FOR BEER TRIVIA CONVERSATIONALISTS

The Stubby

➪ a squat, wide-girthed, brown-glassed, reusable beer bottle in common usage across Canada between 1962 and 1983.

Two opinions as to what finished off the stubby:

➪ Market researchers, hired for insight into how to attract more female beer drinkers, discovered a preference for um, long-necked, American-style bottles over the, uh, stubby.

➪ Competition from new microbrewed brands in more attractive non-standard moulded bottles.

Moving along

➪ Americans equate Canadian higher-alcohol-content beer with moonshine.

- ➪ In general, Canadian beers are brewed to a golden colour, American brews to a pale yellow hue.
- ➪ Americans measure alcohol content by weight (abw), Canadians by volume (abv).
- ➪ An American beer with 4 % abw equals a Canadian brew at 5 % abv.
- ➪ There's no connection between a brew's colour and its potency: colour is a result of toasting malted barley.
- ➪ Unpasteurized beers offer fresher flavour and more carbonation.
- ➪ "Seasonals" are beer styles that complement one of the four seasons.
- ➪ The rule on calories in brews: the higher the alcohol content, the higher the calorie count.
- ➪ Number of calories in a 5 % alcohol content beer: 150–165
- ➪ Number of calories in a "lite" beer: 70–100
- ➪ Can beer claim health food status?

Beer contains:

1) 13 grams of carbohydrates
2) zero fat or cholesterol
3) 25 milligrams of sodium
4) proteins
5) calcium
6) potassium
7) phosphorus
8) vitamins B, B2, B6

- ➪ The best way to clean that empty beer glass: straight hot water rinse and air dry. Towelling leaves unsightly lint and oily streaks.
- ➪ Beer's connection with the rule of thumb: pre-thermometers, brewers dipped their thumbs into the mix to ascertain the correct temperature for adding yeast. If too chilly, the yeast wouldn't grow, too steamy, and it'd die.

▶ What is behind brown or green glass bottles: darker glass keeps direct light out of the bottles so as to keep in freshness and prevent spoilage.

▶ With proper care, the shelf life of beers and ales held at eight to thirteen degrees Celsius and out of direct sunlight is three months.

- ➪ Origin of the term "draught beer" means "pull," referring to the task of the Percheron breed of draught horses hauling beer wagons to taverns before the advent of motorized trucks.
- ➪ Origin of "growler": a metal bucket with a fitted lid used (often by children) on beer runs from local taverns.

Brew clues: what goes with what for the discerning host and hostess

a) With pork or poultry, serve a malty lager.
b) With fish, a nice pilsner will do splendidly.
c) With shellfish, there's nothing better than a decent stout.
d) With red meat, it's the full-bodied ales you'll want.
e) If you're serving pasta or pizza, you've got to have malty amber ales.

BEER

➪ For an ale cocktail before dinner, boldly challenge your taste buds (and your guests) with an "ale flip." The recipe:

1) one pint of ale
2) crushed ice
3) one raw egg
4) shake, don't stir
(Cleanse the palate with a mittful of taco chips.)

➪ Keggers: social functions where beer is provided by the keg(s).

Cock ale, the worst beer... ever, was made by:

➪ skinning, gutting, boiling, and crushing a young bird;

➪ mixing the meat with raisins, mace, rosemary, cloves, dates, and honey;

➪ placing the "mash" into a canvas bag;

➪ immersing the sack in a keg of ale for one week; and

➪ pouring a glass.

The late blues great Dutchie Mason's number one rule for bar bands:

➪ always stay two drinks behind your audience.

THE STORY OF SPRUCE BEER

In eighteenth century Nova Scotia's culture of drinking, spruce beer drove the dances of rural farmers and strived to numb (or cheer up) the brutish lives of garrison soldiers. A punishing beverage, spruce beer was brewed from a recipe comprised of spruce tips, or spruce shoots, mixed with hops, yeast, water, and (a small mercy) molasses.

From 1759

The Daily Order for the Highland Regiment in North America: "Spruce beer is to be brewed for the health and conveniency [sic] of the troops which will be served at prime cost. Five quarts of molasses will be put into every barrel of Spruce Beer. Each gallon will cost nearly three coppers."

- ⇨ "The cup that cheers but not inebriates" is a non-alcoholic version of spruce beer (akin to root or ginger beer).
- ⇨ Alcoholic and non-alcoholic spruce beers depend on the quantity of molasses used.
- ⇨ Homebrews of spruce beer loosened inhibitions at farm dances. The men folk imbibed; the womenfolk abstained; a good time was had by all, half of them would be told.

A PASSAGE FROM *HISTORY OF NOVA SCOTIA*:

The Second Siege of Louisbourg, 1758

"At Halifax, spruce beer was the big commodity and thought to be a very good beverage for the men. Captain John Knox set out a recipe for it: 'It is made of the tops and branches of the spruces-trees, boiled for 3 hours, then strained into casks, with a certain quantity of molasses; and, as soon as cold, it is fit for use.'"

While encamped at Halifax, the soldiers drank copious quantities of spruce beer. "The allowance was two quarts per day to each man, or 3 gallons and a half per week, for which he paid seven pence New York currency."

Biologists have discovered spruces, indeed all conifers, to be abundant in flavonoids commonly known for their antioxidant activity in combating free radicals thought responsible for maladies ascribed to the aging process and the onset of major diseases.

WHY IT'S IMPORTANT TO HAVE A GOOD HEAD ON A BEER:

- it governs the release of carbonation;
- it ensures a tippler gets consistent flavour;
- it scores big in presentation points; and
- it bespeaks of a well-made beer.

THE SPRUCE BEER TASTE TEST

Telling descriptions from brave modern (foolhardy?) samplers

"I've tried it once before. It takes superhuman will and much prayer to even get my nose near this stuff. It smells like Vick's Vaporub."

"The flavour (if that is the right word for self-inflicted torture of this depth) is pine and menthol. If you ever wanted to lick a pine tree, here's your chance."

"After 2 years of aging in the refrigerator, it is now one of the most refreshing, light summer beers I've ever tasted."

Taste, as in comedy, is so, so, subjective.

ALERT THE PUBLIC

Six thousand years ago when enterprising Sumerians in Mesopotamia discovered beer brewing, some producer in a Hanging Beer Garden of Babylon must have opened a discussion over a meal with his associates in the business to generate ideas for ways of moving product. Somewhere, in the midst of the brainstorming, a bright-eyed Babylonian might have blue-skied: What if we were to lure customers with a catchy one-liner brand slogan?

> ▶ The fear of an empty glass is called cenosillicaphobia.

What followed—if indeed this scenario ever happened—is anybody's guess. However, if it did, grim-faced government regulators would have stepped in with restriction edicts. Like this one, centuries later, from the government of Nova Scotia.

Nova Scotia Liquor Commission Advertising Regulations

> "Brand advertising shall not deal with the use and consumption of beer and wine generally, but shall be designed to draw attention to one or more brands of beer or wine by use of language descriptions of those brands."

As we well know, beer advertising slogans need something special to hook eyes and weary ears bombarded 24-7 by aggressive marketing. The best ad lines entered the lexicon of daily usage with a staying power well beyond that of even the cleverest TV advertising. In the U.S., it would take an advertising Shakespeare to best Budweiser's classic, "This Bud's For You." In Canada, the standout has to be Alexander Keith's pithy phrase, "Those Who Like It, Like It A Lot." Enduring. Memorable. Timeless. Like Nova Scotia itself.

WINE

REVELATION IN A BOTTLE: NOVA SCOTIA'S VIN NOT-SO-ORDINAIRE

Oenophiles rejoice. Jitters be gone. Winemaking in Nova Scotia is set to trash a stubbornly held convention that this province cannot produce very good, if not exceptionally fine, table wines. It's taken years and years of trial and error, surmounting harsh weather setbacks, solid research from provincial grape scientists, and a dogged determination to get to this point of success. No more can grumblebunny wine snobs sniff disdainfully at Nova Scotia wines. Nova Scotia's viviculture and wineries—no idle boast or brag here—have arrived, wine lovers: you can now enjoy, in Voltaire's words, "the divine juice of September." Remarkable, considering the rather tortuous journey of development it's taken to get here.

Before relating the Nova Scotia vineyard and winemaking story, some backgrounder wine lore:

⇨ About 4000 to 3000 BC, Turkestanians, swilling fermented juice from squashed grapes left lying around in their fields, discovered themselves giggling and happy and wanting more, maybe with a little cheese on the side.

⇨ In 1683, French monk Dom Pierre Perignon spent his downtime from praying in the Champagne Monastery inventing alcoholic beverages; one in particular, a blending of white wines that he kept tightly corked in bottles, retaining carbon dioxide, made the wine bubbly.

⇨ Louis Pasteur (of pasteurization fame) discovered and revealed a micro-organism crucial for souring wine in 1863.

In Nova Scotia four hundred years ago, give or take a month or two:

- French explorers and colonists clambered ashore in Nova Scotia, lugging with them cases of European wine.
- Nova Scotia is thought by some historians to be one of North America's first sites for grape cultivation from vines brought from the Old Countries.
- 1606 to 1607: Historian and Parisian lawyer Marc Lescarbot called Port Royal home.

From Lescarbot's *History of New France*:

> "Each man in Port Royal enjoyed 3 half pints of good and pure wine a day. This lasted as long as we were there, save that then those who came to fetch us, instead of bringing us supplies, had aided us to empty our casks...we were forced to reduce the ration to a pint."

WINE

A FIRST

New France reports, circa 1611, made the claim that a settler by the name of Louis Hebert plugged grapevines in the ground along the Bear River near Port Royal, thus planting (rousing drum roll here) Canada's first vineyard.

MAYBE NOT

Trouble is, Hebert returned to France in 1607 and did not set foot in North America again until 1617, at which time he rooted himself in Quebec. Enter Isaac de Razilly, the father of Acadia, in 1632.

DE RAZILLY: THE BIO

- ➪ Born and raised in the Loire Valley.
- ➪ An esteemed knight of the Order of Malta.
- ➪ A respected naval captain.
- ➪ A competent and benevolent governor charged with reclaiming Acadia for France.
- ➪ Carved out the capital of New France, namely Fort-Ste-Marie-de-Grace (currently LaHave, Nova Scotia), a starter colony of three hundred men.

From a de Razilly letter dated August 16, 1634, and written at Petite Rivière, to Marc Lescarbot back in France:

> "I have planted vines as they do in Bordeaux which have come along very well. Vines grow here naturally. The wine made from them has been used to celebrate mass. What would they be like if they were cultivated?"

- ➪ de Razilly's question is left unanswered when, in 1636, he dies.
- ➪ The colony moves to Port Royal, abandoning de Razilly's wine-growing efforts in the region.

A MYSTERIOUS SIGHTING OF THE ALIEN GRAPE KIND

French explorer Nicolas Denys, scoping out an area bordering the Northumberland shore near Pictou, reported:

> "The large river is straight in the entrance; boats go seven or eight leagues up it, after where there is met a little island covered with the same woods, and with grape vines, and above which one cannot go higher towards its source except with canoe."

⇨ Botanists say grapevines were not native to Nova Scotia, so what was Nicolas Denys reporting on then? Wild vines? Not possible. So botanists say.

WINE

Here's one good explanation for their existence. LaHave "lies inland from productive fishing banks where hundreds of vessels from Europe catch cod. Fishermen, ashore to dry their catch, may have left seeds of grapes gathered further south."

Before de Razilly assumed duties as colony leader, French settlers traded with the Mi'kmaq living in the LaHave area. Their chief, Messamouet, might be fingered as a culprit for the presence of the wild vines. He had been to France—fabled land of grapes and vines—in the 1580s. Might he have brought back the tasty fruit and a vine as a souvenir of his trip? C'est possible.

Marc Lescarbot noted that he had seen vines growing in the lower Saint John River Valley; 125 kilometers, it was pointed out, "as the crow flies from LaHave." Was it not logical, the line of thought played out, that seeds were transported by migrating birds in their digestive tracts and "released" in New France (Nova

Scotia)? The fall migration route runs in an eastward then southward direction.

However it happened, vines took root in Nova Scotia.

SCENE FROM A FEAST IN THE MID-1630S

Our intrepid French chronicler, Nicolas Denys, jotted down details of a culinary blowout at a logging camp near the mouth of Lunenburg Harbour:

> "I had de Razilly enter a hall which I had built, covered with branches, where he found a table very well furnished, with pigeon soup, with wild geese and brant. To this course there followed another of brant and of teal, and to that, a third of large and small snipe, and plover in pyramids. White wine and claret were not wanting at this little feast, so that Monsieur de Razilly and all his retinue were very well pleased, as indeed were my own men, who hoped that Monsieur de Razilly would come often to see them."

IN AN EARLY 1700S ACADIAN GARDEN

- No interest in large-scale vine plantings among the growers.
- Harvested grapes graced tables as finger fruit.
- Acadia's governor imported barrels of his wine preferences from France and nibbled grapes from local gardens.

⇨ The Acadian expulsion in 1755 left the vines to fend as best they could on their own: their fate was not recorded.

Partying like it's 1787:

Notes from a regimental dinner at the Halifax barracks with Prince Billy, one of King George III's rascalian sons, in attendance. The prince, twenty-one, a captain in the Royal Navy in command of the frigate *Pegasus*, was a hyperactive ruddy-faced rake whose unusually pointed head had awarded him a nickname of Coconut Head. Also present were the lieutenant-governor, a general, and a commodore.

Here is the recorded account by a young subaltern of the garrison named Dyott:

> "The Prince took the chair himself and ordered me to be his Vice. We had a very good dinner and he sent wine of his own, the very best claret I ever tasted. We had the Grenadiers drawn up in front of the messroom windows to fire a volley in honour of the toasts. As soon as the dinner was over he began. He did not drink himself, but he took care to see that everybody filled, and he gave 23 bumpers without a halt. In the course of my experience, I never saw such fair drinking. When he had finished his list of bumpers, I begged leave as Vice to give the Superior, and recommended it to the society to stand up on our chairs with three times three, taking their time from the

WINE

> Vice. I think it was the most laughable sight I ever beheld to see our Governor, our General and the Commodore all so drunk that they could scarcely stand on the floor, hoisted on their chairs each with a bumper in his hand; and three times three cheers was what they were afraid to attempt for fear of falling. I then proposed His Royal Highness and a good wind whenever he sailed with the same ceremony. He stood at the head of the table during both these toasts and I never saw a man laugh so in my life. When we had drunk the last, the old Governor desired to know if we had any more, as if he once got down he would never get up again. HRH saw that we were pretty well done and walked off. There were twenty dined. We drank 63 bottles of wine. If the Prince did not drink on this occasion it was not from sobriety, for drinking and wenching were his pet diversions. Perhaps he had some amorous engagement for the later hours."

"Halifax was full of naughty women," a historian of the times reports, "ranging all the way from the unwashed sluts of Barrack Street to the elegant wife of Surveyor-General of the King's Woods, Mr. John Wentworth, and Billy knew them all."

EARLY VITICULTURALISTS

In the early 1800s, British settlers picked up the viticulture slack. One of these, a certain Charles Prescott, imported vines, enabling him to cultivate Isabella grapes on his Starr's Point acreage in the eastern Annapolis Valley. (Prescott doubled up as a pioneer of the Annapolis Valley apple industry.) Another stand-out vineyard pioneer around the mid-1800s was William Cunard. If that name rings a bell, it should. William's pater was none other than Sir Samuel

Cunard of Cunard Steamship Company Limited, which dominated "the Atlantic passenger trade with liners such as Lusitania and Mauretania." William Cunard's vineyard raised large quantities of Black Hamburg Muscatel grapes, which are still grown as table grapes. Lunenburg County growers in the 1850s clung to the Massachusetts-developed Diana variety of grape, finding great satisfaction with its early ripening characteristic, zesty flavour, and longevity after picking.

"Prior to the 1960s, no one concerned themselves with grapes for commercial wine purposes," said Dr. Donald Craig, who evaluated grape cultivars at the Dominion Experimental Farm in Kentville, Nova Scotia, from 1913 to 1983.

WINE

PROVINCIAL WINEMAKING: THE BEGINNING

➪ Nova Scotia's first commercial winery was started in Kentville in 1941. Chipman's Apple Products, renamed Chipman's Wines Limited, offered only fruit wines.

➪ Abby Wines Limited debuted in Truro in 1965, and later, as Andre's Wines (Atlantic), bought out Chipman's in 1983, and shut down their Kentville winery.

➪ Grapes imported from California, Ontario's Niagara Peninsula, and British Columbia comprised the juice basis for Andre's Wines.

➪ G. N. Baldwin, Andre's chief winetaster, visited the Kentville Research Station for a look at its vineyards, yields, and juice data, and concluded that, as of 1965, "there's nothing of interest to Andre's."

➪ In Dartmouth, T. G. Bright and Company opened its plant

doors in 1985 to "bottle finished wine produced outside Nova Scotia" and shut its doors in the early 1990s, finished itself.

ROGER DIAL

- In 1966, Dr. Roger Dial, with a degree in political science, sprouted an interest in winemaking while working on modest-sized Californian vineyards.

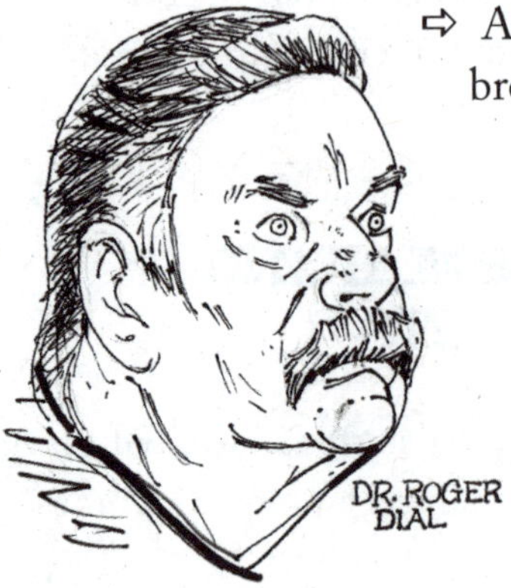

- A Killam political science scholarship brought him to Nova Scotia in 1969.
- With friend Norman Morse in 1979, Dial scooped up some acreage near Grand Pré, and built a five-hundred-foot greenhouse, then the largest of its type in Canada, for ramping up seed propagation.
- He contracted growers to supply the grape crop necessary to produce sufficient quantity of wine to meet commercial needs.
- By 1980 he had netted enough Marechal Foch, Michurinetz, and L'Acadie grapes to commence production.
- Nova Scotia's first-ever farm winery, Grand Pré Wines Limited, Dial's baby, opened in 1981.
- Grand Pré Wines Limited's first wine labels impressed, thanks to their distinctive design by artist Dusan Kadlec.
- These labels adorned the bottles in two hundred cases of Foch offered for sale at the Nova Scotia Liquor Commission.

- ➪ By 1983, brisk and steady demand for Grand Pré wine set the business up for further success.

DIALING: PRODUCTION CLIMBS AND THEN SOME

- ➪ The Michurinetz wine, labelled Cuvée D'Amur, snapped up gold medals at the premier Bristol and New York wine competitions and nabbed the vote in a blind taste competition "organized to choose wines to supply Canada's international embassies" as the best wine.
- ➪ In 1982 Dial, with fellow wine pioneers Hans Jost and Walter Wurther, created the Grape Growers' Association of Nova Scotia: Dial's political science degree payed off and would continue to do so with future wine causes.
- ➪ Suddenly, in October 1987, Black Monday detonated, abruptly reversing the stock market: Grand Pré Wines Limited fortunes turtled.
- ➪ Dial left the production side and advocated on behalf of the Nova Scotia wine industry as a consultant and policy activist.

GRAND PRÉ WINE...UP AGAIN

A Swiss banker, Hanspeter Stutz, flew into Halifax on a business trip. Business meetings are business meetings are business meetings, but, for Stutz, the scenery was something else again. On that fateful trip, he "discovered" Nova Scotia. Back home, after some family discussion, a decision was made. Affairs with the bank were settled. The family packed up effects and emigrated to "Canada's Ocean Playground." Looking for a business opportunity, he found the sadly derelict Grand Pré Wines. It was a fixer-upper, no two ways about it. But Stutz believed he was just the guy with the zest and smarts for the job. Just as a good farmer knows his onions, a savvy banker can spot a good business opportunity when he (or she) sees one.

Convinced he had picked a potential winner, Stutz bought Grand Pré Wines in 1993, and improvements followed. A tasting room was added into the restored farmhouse housing the winery. A restaurant too: Le Caveau. An art gallery. A cobblestone walk with an inlaid granite grape motif as a pathway to the restored farmhouse. And with these additions came a new name: Domaine de Grand Pré. Sagaciously, Stutz and his son Jurg chose to run with grape varieties that thrived in Nova Scotia's flip-floppy weather and immoderate climatic conditions. The payoff? A New York Muscat and an ice wine. And, quel surprise, apple cider—OK, a no-brainer given the area's fame for its apple crop. Domaine de Grand Pré, under the Stutzes' astute directorship, opened in the summer of 2000, a hit showcase for Nova Scotia wines.

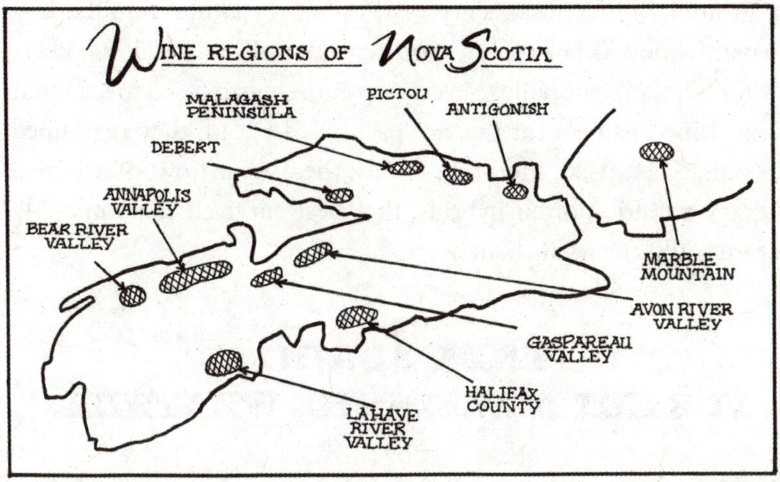

WINE

WEATHER MAPS

Trace out the world's wine-growing regions and what do you find? Nova Scotia teeters at the northern climatic endline for wine-growing. Nevertheless, the province can boast of a rich history of grape growing for wine and other uses. It can only get better. Global warming changes will, for now, enhance the region's ability to support viticulture, but this is a pyrrhic climatic victory when you consider the bigger picture of climate change.

HOWEVER, JUST PRIOR TO HANSPETER

After Stutz's purchase of Grand Pré Wines, lousy growing conditions stretched right through the summer and fall of 1992, weakening vines and leaving them defenceless against a brutal winter five degrees below normal temperatures. All vines were "killed to the ground." The consequence of this "act of nature" resulted in a substantial downsizing of vineyard acreage in 1993 and 1994. Happily for Scotian oenophiles, several resolute souls refused to leg it out of the wine business for greener pastures. Instead, they regrouped and pressed on. Like the Stutz family, these winegrowers switched to grape varieties, often hybrids, that best survived the worst Ma Nature could throw at them.

THEN AGAIN, IT'S NOT ALWAYS THE WEATHER

The Nova Scotia Liquor Corporation's monopoly for selling alcoholic beverages nixed would-be wineries from selling their products directly to consumers. Grape growers stewed. Hans Jost, president of the Grape Growers' Association of Nova Scotia in 1987, was frustrated:

> "In regards to market, the only present outlet is the NSLC stores. To develop a grape industry in Nova Scotia, there must be direct sales from cottage wineries. This is common in all provinces of Canada, in the U.S. and the world. The cottage wineries depend on this outlet for survival."

Later that year, the NSLC adopted the Farm Winery Policy, permitting Nova Scotia wineries to market wines from their own winery stores. Dr. Roger Dial (remember him?) lent his expertise both as a winegrower and a political scientist to the government's drafting of the policy.

THE FARM WINE POLICY

- ⇨ There must be ten certified acres of vines adjacent to the winery.
- ⇨ For each certified acre planted or contracted, a winery is permitted to sell 350 cases of wine.

The minister in charge of the administration of the Liquor Control Act, George Moody, made a wise observation:

> "In retrospect I confess that it did take us, the government, quite a while to get it clear that, for a change, we were dealing with a group that was not looking for a handout. Your demand was for opportunity, not aid."

Shaping up: government policy adds body to the wine industry

- ⇨ In 1991, wineries were permitted to serve food (yay!).
- ⇨ In 1993, the government unveiled a policy to develop a cottage winery (fruit wine) industry.

THE GOODS ON CERTIFICATION

- ▶ Prevents non-bona fide outfits from being able to "hastily plant poorly tended vineyards never to produce a crop" and then sell imported cases of wine "for every acre in the ground."
- ▶ A certified berry crop specialist inspects winery operations to keep standards up.

Cottage Winery Must-haves:

- ⇨ At minimum, ten acres in fruit production.
- ⇨ The ability to output ten thousand to sixty thousand litres of wine a year.
- ⇨ Any wine for sale must contain ninety percent Nova Scotian-grown fruit. (By tradition, farm wineries were permitted to import substantial grape juice quantities or finished wine, which were, at the time, marketed using "lax labelling requirements.")
- ⇨ Nova Scotians noticed postings of blue and white grape cluster signage province-wide in 1993 and the wineries they signalled opened for visitors Sunday afternoons.
- ⇨ 1998 saw the introduction of "local content requirements to give consumers a consistent product with the unique terroir of Nova Scotian vineyards."

The introduction of standards that regulated what was an "official" Nova Scotia wine was a significant step—wine historians even marked it as a tremendous leap forward. In 2000, a small-farm winery policy spawned winery expansion into areas like the LaHave River Valley. Available land limited vineyard sites to lots less than five acres in area. According to regulations under the policy, only two acres of vineyard need to be close to the winery. The big difference

▶ A 1998 rule change dictated a thirty-five percent minimum content of Nova Scotia grapes

▶ In 2006, for wines being sold directly to consumers, there needed to be seventy-five percent Nova Scotia grapes.

between farm wineries and the "two-acre licenses" lay in the wine content standard imposed. Small-farm wineries needed to have ninety percent Nova Scotia grape content in their products.

THE JOSTS

Before immigrating to Nova Scotia, Hans Jost was winning wine-making metals for his Christinehof winery in Germany. In 1970 Jost and his wife, Erna, son, Hans Christian, and daughter, Ellen, settled in Malagash on a seven-hundred-acre spread bordering the Northumberland Strait. The plan was to farm cattle and hogs, the logical reason as to why he brought no vines or winemaking equipment with him from Germany. Strawberries attracted his interest as a possible profitable crop. So, to get the skinny on the plump berry, Jost headed off to the Kentville Agricultural Station. Who did he run into there? None other than research scientist Dr. Donald L. Craig, the very same fellow who evaluated grape cultivars at the Dominion Experimental Farm in Kentville. Twenty-five years after that fateful meeting, Nova Scotia would have its biggest and most prosperous winery. And the book would be closed on Jost's strawberry fields forever. Dr. Craig gave Jost a few of his vines and nearly 750 pounds of grapes to try for winemaking purposes. Jost planted the vines—which wonderfully survived their first Northumberland Strait winter. Impressed, Jost decided in 1979 to dig in four hundred vines of a number of varieties such as Marechal Foch and Seyval Blanc. He didn't end there.

A couple of years later, Jost expanded to four thousand Marechal Foch plantings. In the family garage, with a teensy hand press to squish the grape crop, the Josts turn out six hundred to seven hundred litres of wine per year. A singular drop in the proverbial bucket. Soon Jost output some two thousand litres of wine. But up popped a nightmare: he had no licence to make wine. He worried that he could be charged as a bootlegger, and he moved fast, applying for a licence in 1983. In 1984, Jost's brother Philipp arrived from Germany with a larger press, which the Josts installed in a building they custom built for it.

Hans Jost's son, Hans Christian, spent 1985 away from the family's Nova Scotia enterprise in Geisenheim, Germany, learning the ins and outs of winemaking in a spacious research cellar with esteemed viticulture and oenology professor Dr. Helmut Becker. Over the course of his studies, Jost worked up "special editions of certain wines to retain the uniqueness of grapes grown in different areas of the province." That year, too, Jost Vineyards celebrated its official grand opening and the debut of its ice wine. A year later, the Jost farm winery was licensed to sell its wine on site. Sadly, Hans Jost died in 1988. Jost Vineyards passed into the more than capable and skilled hands of Hans Christian, an "unabashed promoter of the Nova Scotia Wine industry": "There are three things which I want to see happen. First, people have to drink wine, then they have to drink Nova Scotian wine. Finally, they have to drink my wine. If people will help us with the first two, I can take care of the third."

In 2000, Jost Vineyards' 1999 Vidal Ice Wine triumphed as Canada's Wine of the Year at the All-Canadian Wine Championships in Windsor, Ontario.

WINERY MENTIONABLES TO WATCH AND ENJOY

- In 1611 French settler Louis Hebert put in a small vineyard in the Bear River area: location, location, location.
- It was such a good idea that Chris Hawes, who, as a teenager, toiled in the vineyards of the Niagara Peninsula and was later

a neighbour of Dr. Roger Dial at Grand Pré, bought the Bear River site once used by the Kentville Research Station (as well as that of Louis Hebertin 1986). Nothing remained of the former vineyards. What's there today is thanks to Hawes. At its base, the vineyard space sits 60 metres above sea level and ascends at a critical angle up to 140 metres at its upper level.

A neighbour, Hawes discovered, had kept "detailed temperature records for 22 years which showed higher temperature accumulations than any other area of the province where such data exists." Hawes realized this was ideal for ripening vinifera varieties. Bear River Vineyards "came on stream" in 1987, uniquely designed to be "entirely gravity fed with cellars on three levels." Chardonnay, Pinot Noir, Geisenheim 318, Baco Noir, Marechal Foch, Pinot Gris, Seyval Blanc, and "a few odd ones that are only there to make visitors scoff" thrived on Hawes's well-drained, south-southwest exposed vineyards.

AND THEN THE CORKUMS

The Corkums, Suzanne and Doug, planted vines in the Falmouth region of the Avon Valley, home of some of the richest farmland in Nova Scotia. In 1989, the Corkums opened Sainte-Famille Winery, which provincial wine historians categorized as "one of the 'big three'" (Jost and Grand Pré being the other two). Sainte-Famille Winery varietals: Seyval Blanc, Chardonnay, Riesling, L'Acadie, Siegfried and Pollux, and Michurinetz.

2001: YET ANOTHER GOVERNMENT HURDLE TO JUMP

- ⇨ A fifty percent price markup on wine by the Nova Scotia Liquor Corporation put the highest-quality Nova Scotia wines out of contention in provincial outlets.
- ⇨ The Winery Association of Nova Scotia did battle in 2002 with vexatious issues surrounding joint marketing, promotion, and quality standards.
- ⇨ The same year, the Nova Scotia Liquor Corporation called for applications "for the establishment of up to four private wine and specialty stores." Four were chosen, every one in Halifax.
- ⇨ The private outlets sold high-quality Nova Scotia wines with a lower markup: great news for farm wineries who sold directly to these stores.

NOTICING THAT PROMISING SPARKLE IN SCOTIAN WINE

In the spring 2003 issue of *Canadian Grapes to Wine*, editor David Gamble wrote:

> "Nova Scotia is one of the most exciting wine regions of Canada. The Nova Scotia industry is both positioned and poised for a great future."

In the Malagash Peninsula, Hans Christian Jost was on record as saying, "there is more land suitable for viticulture than in the whole of the Niagara region."

- ⇨ Beyond the deeply rooted vineyard emplacements of the Malagash Peninsula, Annapolis Valley, and the Avon River Valley, new wine regions were opening in the LaHave River Valley.

- ⇨ With vinifera showing itself to be hardier than once thought, varieties including Chardonnay, Pinot Noir, and Cabernet Franc were enjoying a surge of popularity in plantings.

A LITTLE BIT OF KNOWLEDGE CAN BE AN ADVANTAGEOUS THING

WINE

You're a dinner guest. There's wine gracing the meal. And wine chat. Perhaps you're well-versed in the world of wine and can more than ably hold your own. Or you are a good actor, very convincing when mimicking the nose, body, and flavour-testing choreography singular to the judging of wines. But suppose you know hardly anything about wines. You could stay cagily mute, moving your head in yes and no gestures in concert with the expert discourse bandied about by your dinner companions. Then again, you could sound adequately erudite on the subject if you have some of the following ready at tongue tip.

Factoids on the three categories of grape varieties cultivated in Nova Scotia

1) The French hybrids

- ⇨ About 1860, pests such as the phylloxera root louse layed waste to European vineyards.
- ⇨ French growers tried to locate and isolate pest-resistant grapes.

- French hybrids were blendings of classic French wine grapes and native American varieties.
- These hybrids, whose quality is known to be generally first-rate, appeared on North American hillsides in the 1930s, and became the foundation of much of the eastern North American wine industry.

2) Vinifera

- These are your classic European wine grapes: name drop Chardonnay and Pinot Noir.

VINIFERA'S DRAWBACKS ARE:

- a sensitivity to cold
- a susceptibility to disease

3) Vitis Amurensis

- Vitis amurensis vines originated in Eastern Russia.
- Roll these variety names off your tongue: Michurinetz and Severnyi
- The Russian grapes, robust and worthy producers, have not matched the overall popularity of hybrids and vinifera.

THE WINE GRAPE LIST

First, your white wine grapes:

1) L'Acadie Blanc (Nova Scotia's signature white grape)
2) Cayuga White (originating in Geneva, New York)
3) New York Muscat (also from Geneva, New York)

4) Seyval Blanc (very hardy and versatile)
5) Vidal Blanc (a late-ripening white French hybrid)
6) Chardonnay (world's most famous grape)

Your red wine grapes:

1) Leon Millot (a cold-hardy French hybrid from Alsace)
2) Luci Kuhlmann (a sister vine to the Millot)
3) Marechal Foch (another sister to Millot and Kuhlmann)
4) Pinot Noir (the holy grail of red wines)
5) Baco Noir (hybrid, hearty, vigorous, can withstand cold)

Favourite Varietals Grown in Nova Scotia:

1) Marechal Foch
2) DeChaunac
3) Baco Noir
4) Leon Millot
5) Seyval Blanc
6) L'Acadie Blanc

THANKS TO OUR WINE INDUSTRY, WE HAVE...

- more sophisticated restaurants
- promotion of healthier lifestyles
- more tourism draws and opportunities
- a healthier rural economy

L'ACADIE AND LEON MILLOT

⇨ The knock against Michurinetz: a vulnerability to mildew.

⇨ Grape growers' non-temperature worries: deer, raccoons, birds. Prevention includes traps, netting, and noise cannons.

⇨ The reason Hans Christian Yost swears that the Gaspereau Valley shines brightest in the province as a grape-growing region: grapes ripen sooner than in the Annapolis Valley.

- ➪ What makes the watersheds of the LaHave River, Petite Riviere, and Medway River unique as a wine-growing area? Drumlins—hundreds of small oval hills throughout the region formed when glaciers last "walked" the province.
- ➪ Vidal Blanc forms the basis for Nova Scotia's award-winning ice wines.

TALK ABOUT CELLARS

For wine collectors, cellars are vaults for storing their racks of liquid treasures, not merely a convenient storage space.

What you should know about a wine cellar:

- ➪ Use wooden racks to store wine: plastic milk crates are a no-no.
- ➪ Locate the rack in a darkish area of a basement where the temperature hovers between 10 to 15 degrees centigrade. This ensures a wine will age slowly (as should we all).

Speaking of temperature:

- ➪ Too much warmth "cooks off a wine's finer characteristics."
- ➪ Too chilly and the wine's maturation process is affected.

Humidity, well, this is a classic *Goldilocks and the Three Bears* situation:

- ➪ too much, the mould dines out on your labels (mould loves damp carpeting)

- too little, your corks dry out and the wine oxidizes
- Always store wine on its side. This keeps the cork wet, thus preventing unwanted shrinkage.

Locate your rack away from:

- furnaces
- stairs
- paints or varnishes
- foodstuffs

AHH, DESSERT AND DESSERT WINES

▶ Dessert wines tend to be sweeter but not to the extent of syrupy sacramental wines, which teeter on the edge of coma-inducing sweetness.

You want to steer wine clear of chemical breakdowns from paints, varnishes, and foodstuffs that can seep through a cork into the wine. A fine wine ought not to have an overriding taste of deck sealant and wood stain to make it special.

THE BIG THREE FRUIT WINERIES

- Telder Berry Farm Winery is found near Nine Mile River: wines crafted from apples, blueberries, cranberries, raspberries, pears, strawberries. Telder Berry offers an apple-spiced Winter Wine (very merry) and a Sangria.
- Williamsdale Winery is situated conveniently in Williamsdale near the Glooscap Trail. It was the first provincial fruit winery to produce tasty sparkling wines from wild blueberries.

⇨ Lunenburg County Winery at Hackmatack Farm, is one hundred acres situated on a drumlin bordered by lakes and woods near the north branch of the LaHave River. Farm crop: blackcurrants, elderberries, raspberries, grapes, and highbush blueberries, from which come the winery's output of dry, medium, and sweet wines and medal-winning dessert wines (palate-pleasers all).

It's impossible to find wine not-the-least-bit interesting. Of course, there are degrees of interest, ranging from enough to avoiding spending good money on the bad stuff, to the all-knowing to-the-edge-of-insufferable oenophile benchmark. If you're someone with wine expertise ambition, you could step up to sommelier—your terribly well-informed wine steward stratum. One such person residing in Halifax is the youthful Mark DeWolf, who graduated magna cum laude from the International Sommelier Guild in 2001. His DeWolf Beverage Consultants caters dinner gatherings where the focus lies in enjoying and experiencing fine wine.

DeWolf also offers "in-home wine education classes." Once instructed, you'll never sniff a screw cap again. For those for whom learning about wines includes instructive bucolic walks through Nova Scotia's winery vineyards, DeWolf, a co-owner of Valley Wine Tours with partner and fellow sommelier Sean Buckland, arranges walkabouts of such wine country beauties as Blomidon Estate Winery, Gaspereau Winery, Jost Vineyards, and Domaine de Grand Pré, among others.

MORE COOL FACTOIDS

▶ although vinifera—Chardonnay, Pinot Noir, and Cabernet Franc—is showing itself to be less delicate than feared, some provincial growers favour the hardy hybrids.

THE LOVELY FINISH

It used to be that when you pored over any map of the world's premier wine-growing regions, Nova Scotia would stand out like a plugged pore on a flea's knee. No longer. Our provincial wine wunderkinds have made Nova Scotia an "exciting wine region, positioned and poised for a great future" with their versions of "the divine juice of September." Will Nova Scotia wines leap with élan onto the world's wine stage and fulfill the promise hinted at back in the 1600s when French immigrants brought vines with them to Nova Scotia for cultivation? Why not? C'est possible.

FINALLY, TO YOUR HEALTH

Good news about drinking red wines. Researchers have been compiling compelling evidence, folks, that red wine drinkers "enjoy a lowered risk of heart disease." Here's how: one set of wine's components, compounds called procyanidins, prevents a natural signal in blood vessel cells that prods blood vessel constriction. Ergo, tipplers, this wine effect means open vessels, fewer blockages, and less risk of heart attack. Cheers.

WHISKY AND MOONSHINE

IF I DON'T GET SOME WHISKY I SURELY WILL DIE

(old song lyric)

Along the whisky trail

➪ In the ninth century, Irish monks—purportedly with Saint Patrick—on a mission to Christianize the Pict pagans in Scotland's rugged hills and verdant glens, brought primitive stills with them.

➪ Before the monks' arrival, the Picts had been brewing an unstable "near beer," heather ale. Using the stills left to them, the Picts learned to distill a much more impressive (and stable) throat-clanger—namely, moonshine.

A commemorative poem by Robert Louis Stevenson

From the bonny bells of heather,
They brewed a drink Lang Syne
Was sweeter far than honey
Was stronger far than wine.

➪ The Picts loved local heather for flavouring various drinks, ales, and whiskies.

➪ They dunked bunches of the plant into boiling water to "sweeten the still" before the first distillation.

➪ Besoms (heather twigs tied to poles to make brooms) were swept around washbacks (wooden mash tubs) by their handlers for cleansing the tubs.

➪ The basis for Scotch whisky: the Picts' heathered-flavoured ales and moonshine.

- Heather whisky is a not-unknown Nova Scotia glass filler, once distilled in yards of homes belonging to Scottish descendants. Check out *Tales of Hamish Iain Iye Haggis, Q.C.* (Halifax, Nova Scotia, Canada) by Janet MacKay and a chapter headed "Hamish at Balmoral Mills."
- It is claimed (by the Scottish and Irish) that Gaelic improves whisky's character and flavour.
- Then again, Gaels insist they invented "Uisce Beatha"—the water of life.
- Gaelic step dancing derived, it's thought, from steadying techniques used to navigate footfalls and goatpaths intact when homebound after way too many drams of "Uisce Beatha."
- In 1494, a Scottish monk named John Cor created the first-ever whisky, delighting his Abbey colleagues. For whatever reason, John Cor kept his beverage production hush hush and his monk mates lush lush.
- Whisky's three basic ingredients: water, yeast, and barley
- The first mention of Scottish whisky: 1496
- The year Scotland's first official whisky distillery opened at Glenlivet: 1823
- In 1773, cargo of Scots disembarked from the *Hector* at Pictou and went off to the Cape Breton Highlands, there to throw up houses, clear trees (and rocks) for farms, dig coal mines, and set up stills.

➪ Their Gaelic language maintained, their clan system successfully transplanted, and their names bespeaking of Celtic origin, Cape Breton would thence be known internationally for its Celtic and Scottish roots.

➪ The Highlanders brought over kilts, pipes, and songs, but most oddly, no recipes for Scotch whisky.

➪ A few lowland Scots farmed near Truro, and their numbers increased as more Scottish immigrants joined them after Scotland's brutal and disastrous Battle of Culloden in 1753.

➪ Moonshine: as much a major spirit and foot lifter at ceilidhs as the infectious music and songs.

➪ Hiram Walker-Gooderham and Worts Limited in Windsor, Ontario, and Sam Bronfman's Seagram cornered legitimate blended Canadian whisky with Canadian Club, Crown Royal, and V.O.

➪ Crown Royal was created in 1939 to mark the visit of King George VI—daddy-dearest to Queen Elizabeth II.

➪ During the Prohibition years of the 1920s, Canadian whisky buddied up with rum for illegal runs into the United States. American imbibers kept up their demand and Canadian distillers got rich quick.

Two colourful Nova Scotia drinking expressions

1) To "shorten up two fingers": making a drinking switch from glasses of beer to splashes of whisky two-fingers deep. That is, the distance between the index finger and the little finger.

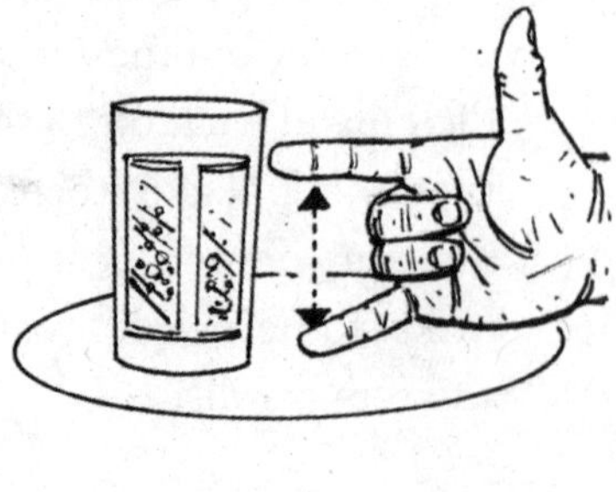

2) "A look into the weekend": beginning weekend drinking on a Thursday.

Proof: the amount of alcohol in a distillate.

⇨ The proof of American whiskies: about 43 to, some claim, a corrosive 110.

⇨ The proof of Canadian whiskies: around 40 (Canadians prefer lighter spirits and longer lives).

EXPLOSIVE INFORMATION FROM THE AMERICAN BARTENDERS' SCHOOL

To suss out a liquor's strength, pioneering distillers blended equal quantities of distillate with (hold your hat) gunpowder. The testers would then fire up a flame and wave it close to the mixture's surface. No burn, the spirit was too weak. Too willing, a column of fire flashed up. A pleasant, even blue flame, stamped the liquor "proved." Hence the term, proof.

Irish coffee ingredients

a) java
b) spoonful of sugar
c) splash of whisky
d) dash of vanilla topped off with whipped cream
(not recommended by the pot or carafe)

⇨ Attention Nova Scotia musicians, particularly blues musicians: Jack Daniel's is not a bourbon but a proper Tennessee whisky.

⇨ Best container for whisky aficionados: the snifter, whose tulip bulb shape excels in capturing whisky's aromas.

WHISKY TESTING AND TASTING

Nosing

Give the whisky a good swirl in a snifter. Pass the glass under your nose. The inside of your schnozz may "prickle, dry up, or slightly burn." These are clues to the liquor's strength. You can judge it to be either medium-bodied or agreeably fiery. Now add just the briefest dash of, preferably, spring water to the whisky. This "softens the nose," and "brings forward" fruit or sweet grain essences. Whiff again. You ought to be able to detect a flowery, fruity, or smoky bouquet. Or a combo of the lot of them. Nosing whisky, experts insist, is a fine way to search out a whisky's intrinsic flavour. Aroma, whisky connoisseurs say, shows off a liquor's "individual personality traits." The nose knows.

Tasting

The sage advice here is to first take the whisky neat (i.e. straight). You're tasting for "a well-defined edge of sophistication." From the initial hit to the tip of the tongue, you'll notice the "alcohol expression," or, shock. Move the liquid across your tongue. Is the liquor sweet? Smoky? Dry? Salty? Is it "creamy with a good flow of toasty wood, almond and caramel"? Do you detect apple? Vanilla? A blend of "butterscotch, heather honey, ground ginger with elongated wood-infused undertones"? Peat? Now, try the whisky with water. Are there fresh fruit notes—especially citrus flavour with a "stronger impression of malt"? This you ought to be able to determine at the back of your palate. Slowly swallow. Wait for the finish. Is it "mellow, softly warm to strong and long-lasting"? Or "rounded, lingering, faintly sweet with just the merest whisper of peat"? Remember to express your judgment tastefully.

▶ Minimum years of ageing, by law, for Canadian whisky: 3

Eyeballing

Hold the snifter up to the light. Peer into the whisky. Is it a lovely golden-amber colour? Or a darker tone? Honey-hued?

All things considered

Sort all of the aforementioned. Work out some colourful descriptives and prepare to pronounce on this matter of taste.

THE GLENORA DISTILLERY STORY

In the mind of Bruce Jardine of Glenville, a hamlet just a little north of Mabou in Inverness County, a hot idea caught fire. Near Glenville lay a narrow and bucolic valley with a cascade called Glenora Falls. And near the falls was MacLennan's Brook, whose flow originates from the Highland snowmelt and a feed from over twenty other brooks. The rock the water courses over is tough granite—the brook's water has none of the minerals in it leached out. If you were to use the water in MacLennan's Brook as a solvent for extracting lots of flavour from barley at, oh say, your distillery, you could scarcely do better. It was well apparent to Jardine. In the late 1980s, stoked with the idea of his own whisky distillery, Jardine bought six hundred acres near the brook, his ideal water source. From 1980 to 1990, he built a distillery in the trad Scottish post-and-beam style: a malt house, kiln, milling production space, warehouses, hospitality facilities, and a pagoda-shaped peat house for "smoking the barley." Then he hastened off to the Isle of Islay, Scotland, the highly regarded Bowmore Distillery's home turf, for guidance and equipment. He returned to Glenville with copper stills, fermentation vats, and the tutelage of a Bowmore's master distiller.

WHISKY HAS BEEN KNOWN IN SONG AS:

- an agent of the devil leading you astray
- an "essential medicine for a broken heart"

With imported Scottish peated barley, MacLennan's Brook water, distillation in Bowmore's copper kettles, ageing in bourbon-soaked oak barrels from Tennessee used (only once) to age Jack Daniel's—Jardine got his new whisky. And a bite from a major, ruinous oversight in his plan: no interim revenue stream. Whisky needs time, lots of it, to age. Unlike his whisky, Jardine aged fast, and plummeted into bankruptcy. Twice. Alas for him there's no third bounce. Jardine suffered the lowest of blows ever to an entrepreneur's psyche. He was forced to bow out.

Meantime, quietly, in Jardine's warehouse, barrels of his whisky seasoned. Enter young lucky Lauchie MacLean in 1994, fresh from a big score in the stock market. In his mid-twenties, MacLean was looking for a cool enterprise to invest his newfound money in. He liked what he saw at MacLennan's Brook. He bought Glenora and its stock of ageing liquor. The 170-litre (45-gallon) barrels were stacked from earthen floor to ceiling. Dusty casks showed darkish stains at the top indicating that some of the spirits had percolated out. (Current master distiller Daniel MacLean says each year Glenora loses about two percent of the liquor he dubs "the angel's share.") From the nearby surroundings, the barrels absorb nuances of spruce, birch, maple, heather, apples, and ocean. This combines with smoky vanilla notes from the Tennessee oak barrels that formerly held Jack Daniel's whisky. (Locals once bought Glenora's used ageing barrels, until the owners found out that the buyers were filling the barrels with water to leach out second-hand whisky.) MacLean faced the same problem that axed Jardine: cash flow. What to do? The solution to this vexing hurdle was at once clever, obvious, and oh-so-sharp.

We all know how much Nova Scotians love their dark, amber, and white rum. MacLean, too. So MacLean and his crack team bottled and sold imported Smuggler's Cove Jamaican rum and peddled near raw alcohol from the whisky stills, a 'shine with a canny name, Cape Breton Silver, fancied up in a pugnacious stubby bottle. To MacLean's surprise and delight, his 'shine rocked—a solid winner with both locals and tourists. His revenue stream burbled. When product did come "on stream," it received enthusiastic reviews, such as this by the whisky world's most respected whisky authority, Jim Murray, on a ten-year-old Glenora Millennium Malt:

- rating: "six out of six"
- comment: "simply gorgeous"

On Glen Breton Rare:

> "Instinct tells me that it will become something of note with the weight to become a malt of character."

Add this assessment by esteemed journalist Jonathan Auerbach in *The Robb Report*, an upscale travel magazine for the enviously rich and famous, on Glenora's eight-year-old whisky: "top rating."

Kilt in a knot, the Edinburgh-based Scotch Whiskey Association, a prickly rampart established for the defense of Scottish whiskies, narrowed its litigious eyes at Glen Breton Rare.

Isn't that name way too close to Glenfiddich, Glenlivet, and Glenmorangie? Burning indignity trumped logic in this case. How could a Scotch whisky drinker miss the maple leaf symbol on Glenora's label? Not to mention the word "Canada"? Or the yawning absence of the words "scotch whisky"? (Unless you figure the consumer is: a) blind drunk, or, b) illiterate.) That Cape Breton glories internationally in its Celtic and Scottish culture, that the distillery is located in Inverness County in the sort of place usually called a "glen," that the company's employees and executive answer to surnames such as MacDonald, McLean, MacKinnon, and MacLeod, counted for nothing.

Surely, dumbfounded watchers wondered, the Scottish whisky industry couldn't be so commercially weak-kneed that when a Canadian micro-distillery put out a very limited number of cases of single-malt whisky, it amounted to a dire threat to their industry's stability. Surely, this was a joke. Not to a shaken MacLean. He was quoted as saying at the time: "I can't pass this off as being frivolous. Glen Breton is really our only economic brand and we've maintained a very successful and loyal following." One newspaper wag, making light of this case, worried in print about the fate of anyone named Glen. The case proved to be a bombastic dud. Wiser heads on the Canadian Trademarks Opposition Board signalled thumbs-down, way down, on the Scotch Whisky Association's arguments. Glenora could retain its Glen Breton label. The Scots threatened to appeal and muttered about the ruling being an affront to international law.

A BANG-UP JOB FROM THE HILLS OF MABOU ENTERPRISE

- ➪ Number of cases sold per year: 2,000.
- ➪ Price for a bottle of Glenora whisky aged ten years: $75–$90.
- ➪ Reason for high prices: the small volume distillery must charge higher prices to cover costs.
- ➪ Price for the first-ever bottle of Glenora whisky: $50,000.
- ➪ Countries clamouring for Glenora products: Switzerland, France, Ireland, Bermuda, Mexico, Japan, Sweden, the United States, and Spain.

RECIPES FOR:

Moscow Mule cocktail
(build over cubed ice in a highball glass)

- ▶ 3 dashes of Angostura Bitters
- ▶ 2 shots of vodka
- ▶ 1 shot of lime juice
- ▶ top up with ginger beer
- ▶ garnish with a lime wedge or a mint leaf

Dark and Stormy cocktail
(in a highball glass filled with ice cubes)

- ▶ 2 ounces of dark rum
- ▶ 3 ounces of ginger beer
- ▶ a lime wedge for garnish

SURE THEY ALL LIKE IT, BUT WHAT ABOUT TORONTO?

Writer Rod Currie tells all in a lead to a Canadian Press story on Glenora, October 12, 2003: "Ritzy Toronto hotels can't get enough of Glenora's single malt whisky."

Other booster descriptives from Currie describing Glenora whisky to *Globe and Mail* readers on May 4, 2002:

- "exotic amber gold";
- "assertive, yet gentle in taste, faintly sweet, displays lots of flavour development."

HOW GLENORA'S WHISKY IS MADE

Jardine's methodology included smoking grains in a pagoda-shaped peat house. No longer. MacLean's enterprise imports lightly peated barley from Scotland for a less smoky note. The pagoda has been "re-purposed" into a small museum and reception area.

Journalist Marie Nightingale reported the stages of the whisky-making process in *Saltscapes*, winter 2003. Here is the condensed version (with additional info from *The Spirits of Canada*):

ALSO ON OFFER AT GLENORA DISTILLERY:

- guest rooms and chalets
- the Glenora Pub
- Celtic music
- a fifty-seat restaurant
- distillery tours

- In huge steel tanks called mash tuns, malted barley is mixed with water.
- The raw liquid (called the wort, a beerlike mash) travels through a heat exchanger that cools it.

▶ Favourite beverage of Glenora master distiller Daniel MacLean: beer.

- The wort flows into large, weathered washbacks—vats made in Scotland from British Columbia fir.
- Yeast is added.
- Fermentation time: 60 hours.
- Liquid goes into the first of two 11,000-litre (2,860-gallon) shiny copper-pot stills and is heated to 80°C.
- Vapour is collected and condensed to a concentrated alcohol. This be yer whisky.
- Liquor is measured for alcohol content before it flows into a spirit still for a second distillation, giving the liquor extra smoothness and purity.
- This process is repeated until the liquid reaches the final spirit receiver and transfer into bourbon-soaked oak barrels for ageing.
- In the warehouses, the barrels are stacked to breathe in ambient, localized "nuances."
- Fumes from leaching rise.
- Whisky in the upper barrels absorbs these fumes and darkens.
- One hundred barrels of whisky are "dumped" together to "marry each other"; in effect, blending the various colours into a warm honey-hue before bottling.

- ➪ Ages of whisky bottled each year: 8, 9, and 10 years old.
- ➪ A worth-the-wait special Glenora: will be available after thirty years of ageing.
- ➪ The last word on Glenora whisky: *Slainte* ("to yer health").

NIGHT MOVES WHEN THE MOON SHINES

"Moonshine can make off with your dignity before you understand."

From the song "*Moonshine Can*" (traditional Newfoundland song):

"I'd like to know how
moonshine's made,"
the Magistrate did say.
"Of yeast cake and molasses, sure that's the proper way
Of yeast cake and molasses, sure that's the cutest plan."
And the Magistrate was happy then, he took me moonshine can.
Now, here's to the man who wrote this song, I'm sure he was not lyin'
And if you wants to know his name, his name be Patty Ryan.
His name be Patty Ryan, me B'y, from Goose Town he belong.
And when moonshine time comes 'round again,
he'll make it twice as strong.

MORE THAN YOU SHOULD KNOW ABOUT MOONSHINE

The basic process

- ➪ Yeast fermenting a sugar source (the mash) produces ethanol (grain alcohol).
- ➪ The alcohol separates from the mash using a still for distillation.

WHAT YOU CAN FIND IN 'SHINE NOT AGED IN BARRELS:

▶ "off" flavours, impurities, toxins—the deadliest being methanol.

Methanol—the dirt nap alcohol

- ➪ Also known as: wood alcohol, wood spirits, methyl alcohol.
- ➪ Properties: volatile, colourless, flammable, poisonous. A distinctive odour milder and sweeter than ethyl alcohol (the drinkable alcohol).
- ➪ What you can do (with care) with methanol: use it for anti-freeze, a solvent, or a fuel.
- ➪ If you happened to swill some methanol from a jug, blindness could occur—if you're lucky; if you're unlucky, death.

BAD MOON (SHINE) RISING:

- ➪ 'Shiners fooled customers of their product's proof content by mixing beading oil or lye into their potion. Bubbles that formed when the container's contents were shaken indicated the hooch's strength, namely, the larger the bubbles and the shorter time they lasted before popping, the higher the proof.

- The flame test: a splash of moonshine in a spoon is lit and, as the theory goes, if it glows with a blue flame, the 'shine's good to drink. If the flame burns yellow, it's tainted.
- More flame test lore: if the alcohol gives off a reddish flame, it's likely a radiator coil was utilized as a still condenser and means there's lead in the alcohol.
- Cautionary 'shine rhyme: "lead burns red and makes you dead."
- What the flame test can't detect: methanol, which will also "make you dead."

MOONSHINE'S ETYMOLOGY

▶ The descriptive term "moonshine" popped up in eighteenth-century English lingo and went on to be known as "moonlight" in nineteenth-century England. Illicit whisky and related spirits were distilled or slipped into England under the light of the moon: ergo, its name. Years later and an ocean away, bootlegged moonshine manufactured in Canada was exported (as in smuggled) for sale and consumption illegally in the era of 1920s Prohibition.

'SHINE SLANG ORIGINS EXPLAINED:

1) "Jakey," according to the Urban Dictionary definition, means a hard-core alcoholic. It's derived, it's thought, from "jake," West Scottish slang for "a drunk."

2) "Canned Heat": a hirsute 1960s white-boys-playin'-th'-blues boogie band. The band name was purloined from Bluesman Tommy Johnson's 1928 composition "Canned Heat Blues," which refers to guzzling the alcohol from Sterno, a.k.a. canned heat—a fuel in gel form.

STERNO: INSIDE THE CAN OF A "HEATING SOLUTION FOR OVER 100 YEARS"

Sterno is a solid gel substance, invented circa 1900, and concocted from ethanol, methanol, water, an amphoteric oxide gelling agent, and a dye that gave it a distinctive pink colour. It is fashioned to be burned straight from the can.

➪ Sterno's flame is virtually invisible.

➪ Company chemists used methanol to denature the product, the idea being to make Sterno too toxic to drink. Undeterred by prevention through chemistry, alcoholics mix Sterno with water or other liquids, such as grain alcohol, before squeezing the sodden glop through a rag or a sock to extract alcohol they dub "canned heat," "squeeze," or lovingly, "pink lady."

From the Whitney Pier Museum. Donelda MacDonald reports:

> "The still shown here was once used to boil mash to make moonshine in Whitney Pier. It was found by a passerby near Inglis Lake, a once popular swimming and recreation spot in Whitney Pier. Although illegal, moonshine has always been part of Cape Breton culture. Known locally as 'Cape Breton Silver' (see earlier Glenora Distillery story for a connection), this potent brew often appeared when a gathering was well underway. One local method of testing its quality has been to pour a small amount of moonshine onto a spoon and light it on fire. The bluer the flame, the better the moonshine. [But we already knew that.] Historically, 'shine sales have been part of the underground economy and a living strategy by working-class people supplementing an otherwise low income."

As long as there are back woods, ready thirsts, and kitchen parties, it stands to reason that, in the still(s) of the night, moonshine will shine on.

FROM *I AM A CAPE BRETONER*:

▶ "Moonshine, if drunk well, will give you the shits."

TEA AND COFFEE

TATTLE TEA TALES

Mark Twain, curmudgeon and fabled author of American classics *Tom Sawyer* and *Huckleberry Finn*, once drawled, "Tea is an affront to luncheon and an insult to dinner." Taking a dissenting view is a 1925 song lyric by Irving Caesar: "Tea for two, and two for tea, and me for you, and you for me." What's the story behind the second-most consumed beverage in the world (after water) that could instigate such opposites of opinion? Let's start with the contentious beginning. Here's one offered by certain historians.

In his garden, Chinese emperor and Son of Heaven, Shang Yeng (circa 2,700 BC), was nursing back a cup of hot water. A few leaves from a Camellia sinensis bush landed in his cup. On a whim, the intrigued emperor raised the cup to his lips and took a sip of "tea." Across his kisser spread a smile. He liked it. And so, accordingly, tea began. That's one take. Here's another:

- In 2,700 BC another emperor, Shen Nung, cited himself as the discoverer of tea's virtues.
- In any case, the Chinese got a head start, enjoying tea long before the rest of the world learned about the beverage. The mid-sixteenth-century name for the beverage "tcha" or "tay," from the Cantonese pronunciation of the Chinese word for tea, was adopted by the Japanese and the Portuguese.
- Chin Hung, a scholar and physician back in 2,200 BC, reputedly (and soberly) said: "Tea is better than wine, for it leadeth not to intoxication, neither doth it cause a man to say foolish things and repeat thereof in his sober moments."
- A famous Chinese sage of the Tang Dynasty (AD 780), Lu Yu, wrote: "Tea tempers the spirit, harmonizes the mind, dispels las-

situde and relieves fatigue; awakens thought and prevents drowsiness and lightens and refreshes the body and clears the perceptive faculties."

- The tea plant itself is native to Assam, India, and was brought to China prior to 2,600 BC in the silk and oriental merchandise trade between India and China.

COMMENT OF THE TIMES:

▶ "[Tea] had yet to become the friend of the poor as well as the consolation of the rich."

- In the 1300s Venetian traders like Marco Polo got wind of the existence of tea, yet Polo preferred the Chinese inventions of gunpowder and spaghetti to dazzle his patrons back home.
- It was left to Dutch traders in 1610 to introduce tea into Europe.

The first European written mention of tea: 1635 by an Englishman named Wickham to a chap named Eaton, a rep of the East India Company (incorporated in 1600) at Macao, near Canton. Wickham asked Eaton for "a pot of the best sort of chaw."

- A dissenting view from another European: in 1633 a German Doctor Olearius insisted tea was "a black water of acrid taste."
- By mid-century, tea spread to England and its American colonies.
- Price for tea when first sold in England: ten pounds the pound weight (i.e. ten pounds for one pound of tea).

➪ Portuguese princess and tea fanatic Catherine of Berganza married Charles II and began the tradition and custom of afternoon tea.

➪ The first seventeenth-century English merchant to sell and retail tea: Thomas Garway, tobacconist and coffeeman in Exchange Alley. He recommended tea as a curative for any ills.

➪ A June 20, 1667, entry from Samuel Pepys, fabled diarist: "Home and there found my wife making tea, which Mr. Pelling the Apothecary tells her is good for her cold."

➪ Prices eased back as imports increased.

➪ Proprietors of London taverns hit upon the practice of soaking the leaves and storing the liquid in barrels for drawing, like pulling beers and ales.

➪ Soon, tea actually competed for tavern popularity with beer and ales.

➪ Then, in 1660, a special (as in outrageous) tax of eight pence was slapped on each and every imported pound of tea.

➪ By 1683, tea's popularity transcended every class level, and was punishingly taxed even further.

TEA WAS SO EXPENSIVE AT SIXTEEN TO FIFTY SHILLINGS A POUND THAT:

▶ Deemed a costly luxury, it was kept in "caddies" [small metal boxes] under lock and key.

▶ It was presented as a costly gift to princes and other important people.

▶ It was only used as "a Regalia in high society entertainments."

- ➪ What happens when a commodity is taxed thusly? Smuggling, friends, smuggling.
- ➪ In the colonies, much of the tea landed came courtesy of neighbourhood pirates "infesting the West Indies."
- ➪ Off Madagascar, buccaneers plundered heavily laden Europe-bound merchant ships, their holds chock-a-block with spices, silks, and, yum, tea.
- ➪ Secretive bases in the West Indies warehoused the plundered cargos.

Dr. Samuel Johnson (1709–1784), lexicographer and renowned man of English letters, on tea:

> "I am a hardened and shameless tea drinker who has diluted his meals with only the infusion of this fascinating plant. With tea I amuse the evening, with tea I solace the midnight and with tea I welcome the morning."

- ➪ From its incorporation in 1600 until the company's charter was withdrawn in 1834, Britain's East India Company (a.k.a. the John Company) monopolized the tea trade.
- ➪ Parliament's Tea Act of 1773 empowered the East India Company to set up field offices in the colonies and the right to levy

TEA & COFFEE

duties "upon arrival of product in American ports."

- ➪ The "crowning outrage": the company levied a tax of three pence per pound on off-loaded tea, which shocked and appalled tea-mad colonists.
- ➪ Firebrand Samuel Adams "fired the embers of disquietude amongst Bostonians," convincing stevedores to refuse to unload the East India Company's ships and warehouse their cargos.
- ➪ On December 16, 1773, men in disguises boarded the vessels and dumped tea into the harbour.
- ➪ The Boston Tea Party, as it became known, sparked the American Revolution.

Sympathy with the Americans existed in Nova Scotia. From *Halifax, Warden of the North* by Thomas Raddall:

> "A great stack of hay, gathered at the port for shipment to Gage's cavalry in Boston last year, had been fired and destroyed. A shipment of taxed tea, spurned by Massachusetts and landed in Halifax, had aroused a strong agitation for a boycott if not another Boston Tea Party. Council had to take strong measures. Prominent Halifax merchants: William Smith, Alexander Brymer, John Fillis, Malachi Salter were suspected of complicity in these and similar matters. Three were members of the Nova Scotia Assembly, which made suspicion darker still. No proof of complicity, they escaped prosecution."

- ➪ That powerful "colossus of rum," Joshua Mauger, used his vaunted "coils of business and political control" to secure Great Britain's grip on Nova Scotia's loyalty.

- The eventual reason for the East India Company's charter withdrawal: the price of tea. Tea "is a question for every Englishman's breakfast table."
- Monopoly in the tea trade, the government concluded, was "a bad thing for the consumer."
- New tea companies (including some flim-flam businesses) sprang up, including the India Tea Company, which shipped its first consignment of 488 pounds of tea to London in 1839. The tea was sold at auction in Mincing Lane, fetching from three to seven dollars per pound.
- The Assam Company formed and subsequently produced eight to nine million pounds of tea annually.
- By 1840, six thousand pounds of tea voyaged to London.
- Clipper ships, with bows raked forward and their masts raked aft, "ran off" with the tea trade.
- On one voyage, fast cargo-carrier *Cutty Sark* ate up 363 miles in a day.
- A primary tea port in colonial days: Halifax.
- First direct tea shipment to the Maritimes: 6,517 tea chests from China aboard the *Countess of Harcourt* in 1826.

J. E. MORSE'S TOP EIGHT TEA PRODUCERS BY VOLUME, 1879–1937

- Northern India
- Ceylon
- China
- Java
- Japan
- Southern India
- Sumatra
- Formosa

THE STRANGE TALE OF "PAINTED TEA"

In 1853, the British were mad for green tea. The greener, the better. Robert Fortune, a British botanist and traveller employed in the tea trade of the era, logged this:

> "By one of those perverse tastes which obtain amongst us, our non-tea purchasers betrayed a strong predilection for a certain colour. 'Foreigners' said the Chinese, 'like to have their tea uniform and pretty.' So they poisoned the herb to gratify the ridiculous tastes of Europe and America (including colonial style-conscious Nova Scotians) for bright green, just as many of our pickle-makers poisoned the pickle. Tea growers threw in a blue substance, which appeared to be salts of copper, and they mixed with it a quantity of gypsum. They never thought of drinking this tea themselves, but the more gypsum and blue they could communicate to the plant, the higher the value in the eyes of their best customers, and the dyeing process accordingly goes in China to an alarming extent."

Similarly, at the turn of the twentieth century, fashionistas drank another green beverage, absinthe, that contained anise

LU YU, CHINESE SAGE (DIED IN 804), ON THE SUBJECT OF TEA:

▶ "The best quality tea must have creases like the leathern boot of Tartar horsemen, curl like the dewlap of a mighty bullock, unfold like a mist rising out a ravine, gleam like a lake touched by a zephyr, and be wet and soft like a fine earth newly swept by rain."

and wormwood, the latter a deadly, bitter, dark-green plant oil. What people will do for fad and fashion is mind-boggling. The painted tea fad peaked, though, and emerald tea became as rare as chocolate teapots.

TEA CULTIVATION

- ⇨ Botanical plant family: Camellia
- ⇨ If pruned: an evergreen shrub
- ⇨ Left unpruned: a twenty- to thirty-foot tree
- ⇨ Where the finest grades of tea were grown: up on the higher altitude slopes of Darjeeling in sight of the Himalayas
- ⇨ Days apart that freshly formed leaves called "flushes" for "plucking" appear: eight to ten
- ⇨ Leaves that make the finest grades of tea: the smallest
- ⇨ Orange pekoe "indicates the size of the graded leaf—not the quality."

TEA & COFFEE

A DESCRIPTION OF THE TRADITIONAL MANUFACTURE OF PURE TEA:

"Gathered leaves from which green tea is to be made are brought from the plantation, and spread out thinly on small bamboo trays in order to get rid of the moisture. In 2 hours, the leaves are dry. They are then thrown into roasting pans, rapidly moved about and shaken up. Affected by the heat, the leaves make a crackling noise, become moist and flaccid, and yield considerable output of vapour. In this state they remain 5 minutes, when they are drawn quickly out and placed upon the rolling table. (The fundamental object of the roll is the release of the theine and tannin secreted in separate cells, and thereby allow these essential properties of the beverage to mingle freely until stabilized by the firing process.) Men take their stations at the rolling table and divide the leaves among them. Each takes as many as he can press with his hands and compacts them into the form of a ball. The ball is rolled upon the table and greatly compressed, forcing out the last remaining moisture and giving the leaves the necessary twist. The leaves are then shaken out upon flat trays and carried once more to the roasting pan where they are kept in rapid motion by the hands of the workmen. In an hour and a half, the leaves are well dried and the colour is fixed."

TEA FACTS

- Four pounds of plucked leaf will become one pound of dry tea.
- Number of pounds of charcoal used to cure one pound of tea: 1.
- Number of ordinary teacups of tea to be had from one pound of tea: 280.
- Number of cups of coffee from one pound of coffee: 30–40.
- Orthodox tea: use the top two leaves of each plant—the best quality tea leaves (tea junkies claim).
- Tea contains more caffeine by weight than coffee does (so what's all this about a nice, relaxing cup of tea then?).
- But there is less caffeine per cup of tea than in a cup of coffee.

TEA TERMS DERIVED FROM THOSE USED CENTURIES AGO IN CHINESE TEA FIELDS:

- *pekoe*: the peach-fuzzy bloom and the first (highest) leaf on a young shoot from which "the best tea is made."
- *souchong* (Chinese term for small plant): the second leaf and half of the third from a tougher stretch of the stalk.
- *congoo* (Chinese for labour): the large, coarse fourth leaf used to produce "common tea."

Black and green tea:

Both come from the same plant—the difference occurs in the process of curing the leaves. Black tea is created when the leaves are left to ferment for several hours (transforming into a bright coppery colour), then fired in dryers, without being exposed to fumes or gases, until they attain their distinctive blackish colour.

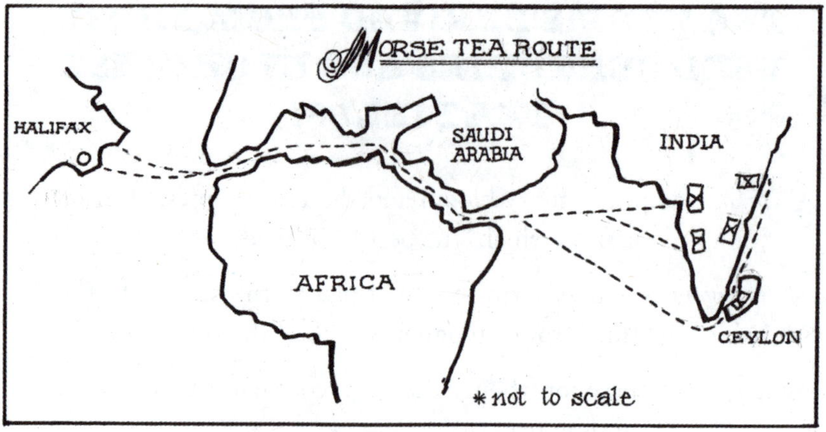

MORSE'S TEA ROUTE

From 1879 to 1937, J. E. Morse and Company was no ordinary little tea-shop. It thrived as a very important Nova Scotia tea merchant and manufacturer. When Nova Scotians thirsted for a "dish of tea" (an expression often used), "it's Morse of course, the beverage that picks you up but never lets you down" (yet another Morse slogan). Taking its business seriously, J. E. Morse and Company was the first tea firm in the Dominion of Canada to dispatch a tea rep from the company abroad to the primary tea markets. With canny foresight, Morse's management bet large on "the future importance of Empire-grown teas." It was not an uncommon sight to see Morse tea tasters rubbing shoulders with reps from the larger tea companies. Ready for business, taste buds at the ready, the

men from Morse sauntered into a long room with windows facing north "to provide an even light" so that a tea's colour could be carefully judged. A long table with tea samples in airtight tins from various plantations, and marked with the shipment's number, sat in the room. A small teapot and cup fronted each tin. An attendant tumbled a very deliberately weighed quantity

MORSE BLENDS (IN HALF-POUND PACKAGES):

- Bluenose
- Standard
- Orange Pekoe
- Fine Darjeeling

TEA & COFFEE

of tea into the pot, which was then filled with hot water. The tea was allowed to steep for exactly six minutes. At the correct moment, the "liquor" was poured into the cups. To the palates immediately, right? You'd think so, but nope. Instead, the infused tea leaves displayed in the upturned lid of each teapot got the once-over. The leaf exams concluded, the tea tasters moved down the line of cups, slurping and jotting notes from which company reps would base their estimation of the sampled teas' market value. Later, at the big London tea auction, savvy buyers had a pretty good idea of what to bid for which shipment.

J. E. MORSE AND COMPANY—ONCE THE OLDEST TEA FIRM IN CANADA—ADVERTISING SLOGANS:

- "Morse's Standard: The Good Old Family Tea of the Maritimes"
- "Morse's Teas: Quality in Every Cup"

But the tasting routine didn't stop there. When a cargo of tea was off-loaded in Halifax into the Morse waterfront operations in the Morse Building (still extant in the Historical Properties area), tasters took over, in a scene similar to that in the East. This time, however, the goal was to carefully choose the exact leaves for "blending to suit the consuming market." An "educated palate" and a lot of patience were qualifications for the job. Without these assets, the firm couldn't ensure the "uniform flavour, body, strength and colour" its blended tea products' reputations rested on. Blending was no simple task. Sometimes teas from as many as eight to ten different tea gardens (plantations) combined to form a blend. As luck would have it for J. E. Morse, a wowser invention came along to guarantee the firm many happy, sunny, prosperous business days—the invention of metal foil packaging. Before foil, buying bulk tea was dodgy at best for consumers. With foil wrapping, freshness was guaranteed.

This from an old J. E. Morse and Company "Tea Tips" booklet:

> "As shipments arrive they are blended and packed. Expert blenders maintain with exacting standards of quality for which Morse Teas have long been famous. Finally, ingenious machines weigh and seal the fresh blended teas in foil packages, ready to be supplied, through the cooperation of a vast army of grocers, to homes in every village, town and city in the Maritimes."

MORSE TEAS WANTS YOU TO KNOW

- ⇨ Infusion (steeping tea in hot water) extracts three constituents found in tea-leaves: essential oils, alkaloid theine, and tannin.
- ⇨ Essential oils mean essential flavour.
- ⇨ Alkaloid theine gives a drinker's tea mild stimulation, which "lessens fatigue and soothes tired nerves."
- ⇨ Tea "stewed" (allowed to brew too long), results in a bitter flavour.

J. E. Morse's handy-dandy guide for making a great (even award-winning) pot of tea

- ⇨ A must—an earthenware tea-pot, preferably a Brown Betty, which originated in the latter seventeenth century. (Avoid pots made from rubber, cellophane, or a cheap cardboard blend.)

- ⇨ Pour in boiling water and let the pot stand to warm.
- ⇨ Empty the teapot.
- ⇨ Put a precise measure of tea into the pot: a teaspoonful for each person and an additional "one for the pot."
- ⇨ Add freshly boiling water, gently swirling for "exquisite infusion."
- ⇨ Brew for for exactly five minutes, on the dot.

- ⇨ Stir the infusion (any direction is fine and the number of stirs is up to you).
- ⇨ Let stand for another couple of minutes (that's two minutes, friend, for pure perfection).
- ⇨ Pour and prepare for accolades.
- ⇨ Note to the wise and frugal: "high grade teas (J. E. Morse's) prove more economical in use than the cheaper varieties as less needs to be used."

A handy guide to tea-leaf reading: shapes and their meanings from your friends at J. E. Morse Teas:

- ⇨ anchor: found at cup bottom, this means success by water; at cup top, constant love; mid-cup, good luck in business and commerce and money from water.
- ⇨ acorns: at cup top, a foretelling of riches easily gained; cup bottom, recovery from an illness, or if in financial difficulties, assistance is at hand.
- ⇨ basket: standing by itself, expect an addition to the family. If incomplete, you're about to receive news of a broken engagement or postponed nuptials.
- ⇨ boot: if you hold a political position, that's about to change. This is an omen (and not a good one).
- ⇨ cage: near cup top, steady yourself—there's a proposal of marriage in the works; mid-cup, a marriage of convenience (but for whom?); bottom of the cup, your engagement is toast.
- ⇨ crown: smile—there are honours in store. If crowded by other tea leaves, your honours will be beset by difficulties and delays.
- ⇨ egg: consider yourself to be one lucky person. The more eggs the better and the bigger your success.

- fish: you net wealth; if lines lead to the fish, you lose.
- fiddle: good news, happy times, an offer of marriage.
- jug: symbol of excess; turn down all party invitations for a week.
- kettle: cup bottom means quarrels and domestic contretemps; cup top, however, means domestic efficiency, comfort, and happiness.
- ladder: advancement is yours for the climbing.
- lamp: cup top means things once hidden are to be revealed (for good or bad), and lost property will be recovered; cup bottom, a festival will be postponed.

A MOMENT FOR SOME TIMELY TEA REMARKS

- "Make tea not war."
—Monty Python
- "Never trust a man who, when left alone in a room with a tea cozy, doesn't try it on."
—comedian Billy Connolly
- "The tea party is the spa for the soul."
—Alexandra Stoddard
- "Is your tea good yet?"
—a Nova Scotian waitress
- "More hot?"
—a Nova Scotian waitress

- stars: hope and destiny in a cup. Cup top, great fortune and honours are coming to you; many stars clustered at cup bottom means you will have a long life with many troubles.
- tree: a single tree means good health; a forest, your wishes will be gratified.
- umbrella: if closed, your wishes are denied; open, this is cause to run for shelter with friends.
- wheel: smile, an inheritance is about to come.

PERSONALI-TEA

- ➪ Green tea drinkers are those who "demand balance in all parts of life, are 'at one with themselves'; reliable and honest."
- ➪ Oolong drinkers seem self-confident and self-assured: it's an act.
- ➪ Earl Grey drinkers are "delicate, easily bruised but thrive on positive criticism."
- ➪ Darjeeling (the champagne of teas) drinkers are your "conspicuous consumers" with a lust for life.
- ➪ Assam drinkers see themselves as "everybody's friend and good fun to be with."

NOT ONLY ASSAM DRINKERS AND SUGAR USERS HAVE FUN

An unidentified blogger's comment about tea-drinking on the other side of the causeway:

> "I grew up with tea. I liked when my mom went to visit her family and friends in Cape Breton. They would put a little something in their tea. I only realized it when I was older."

▶ Name of an appropriate Cape Breton fiddle tune: "Brew of Tea Jig."

TEA & COFFEE

North Cape Breton tea technique as recalled by United Church minister Doug Pilsworth:

"In North Cape Breton, the tea of choice is King Cole. What they do is, firstly, boil the kettle to warm up the water. Then they pour that into a Pyrex coffee pot and add a couple of tea bags. That's set upon the burner of the stove for about 10 minutes, usually on high. When you can hear the tea bags screaming, it's ready. Then they ask you if you want milk or sugar in that. I haven't met anyone in the Maritimes as yet who warms up the pot, swilling the hot water around, emptying it, putting in the tea, pouring in the water and letting it sit. The people tell me that that makes too cold a cup of tea."

IT'S TRUE (YOU COULD LOOK IT UP)

- Atlantic Canadians drink one-and-a-half times the Canadian average of tea.
- A newspaper notice in the *Cape Breton Post*: "Annual Cape Breton Presbyterian meeting: biscuits, bonnach, oatcakes and tea."
- Another popular tea brand in Nova Scotia households: Red Rose Tea. Red Rose Tea is a Saint John, New Brunswick, brand established in 1894 by Theodore Estabrooks, a local merchant, and M. R. Miles, a tea man extraordinaire from a prominent English tea-taster family.
- The basis for its rich and flavourful taste: Red Rose blends Indian and Sri Lankan teas.

- ➪ In 1929, Red Rose introduced tea bags.
- ➪ Unilever bought out Brooke Bond Canada—proprietors of the Red Rose brand—in 1984, shut down Canadian operations, and moved the Red Rose brand stateside.
- ➪ A defunct Red Rose slogan: "only available in Canada."

FROM *PATHWAYS: RESTFUL MEDITATIONS,* THIS ZEN HAIKU POEM:

"Strange how a teapot
Can represent at the
same time
The comforts of solitude
And the pleasures of
company"

AS FOR J. E. MORSE TEAS

Barbour's of New Brunswick, in business since 1867, marketed King Cole Orange Pekoe tea, another popular household brand in Nova Scotia, and perennial provincial favourite, Morse's Tea.

SEE SEA AND SEA TEA

Bluenose fame evolved into cult status in 1937 when the salt-banker debuted on the tails side of the dime. Corporate interests sat up and took notice. Identifying *Bluenose*'s robust public allure, product marketers set about to pack store shelves with Bluenose products: calendars, milk, paint, skis, underwear. And, of course, Bluenose tea.

NOT YOUR REGULAR CUP OF TEA

Between 1783 and 1812, African-Canadians living in Preston, Shelburne, Brindleytown, and Weymouth brewed teas from hemlock and boxberry, which they sweetened with maple syrup. Traditional African natural curative lore, brought with them to North America, involved boiling the barks of many plants to brew teas to remedy various and sundry maladies. Here in Nova Scotia, some tea makers blended their bark teas with wild ginger, ginseng, sarsaparilla, and plantain (which must have been a whole lot easier to swallow than the healing brew local herbalists cooked up from sheep manure). That was only part one of a potent one-two healing punch. To make certain that a cold stood no chance whatsoever to linger on, and in lieu of the dreaded mustard plaster treatment a few of us can remember, the sufferer's bared chest was slathered with a virus-fighting goop comprised of goose grease and molasses.

IT'S A FACT

- ⇨ Today there are three thousand varieties of tea.
- ⇨ Traditionally "tea" referred to beverages derived from the evergreen shrub Camellia sinensis, from which came black and green tea. Now tea includes infusions made from a number of herbs known as tisanes.
- ⇨ Red tea: rooibos from a South African legume plant.
- ⇨ Red tea contains polyphenols (antioxidants), which have been shown to block damage caused by free radicals to one's DNA and other molecules.

And lastly, this friendly sentiment from an unattributed poet:

"Tea pot is on, the cups are waiting.
Favourite chairs anticipating.
No matter what I have to do,
My friend, there's always time for you."

"COFFEE SHOULD BE BLACK AS HELL, STRONG AS DEATH AND SWEET AS LOVE."

-Turkish proverb

From a Nova Scotia tourist blurb:

> "Halifax is a modern port city teeming with coffee shops. Haligonians love their caffeine. Coffee shops are hangouts, entertainment destinations, gathering places—a way of life for all walks of life including the business and government set. Coffee shops attract everyone. Halifax resembles a European Mecca with sidewalk cafes, both locally owned and international chains."

COFFEE DRIPPINGS

- ➪ Ninety percent of those living in the West over the last three centuries have switched from tea to coffee.
- ➪ Coffee accounts for 75% of all caffeine consumed in North America.

- In any shades of coffee roast, the caffeine content is virtually the same: a smidge less for dark.
- Japan ranks number three in coffee consumption in the world.
- Number of cups of coffee served worldwide per year: 400 billion.
- Number of people employed in various aspects of the coffee business: 20 million.

- Number of ships transporting coffee beans each annum: 2,200.
- Hemp coffee sacks full of green coffee beans tip the scales at 132 pounds.
- Number of beans to fill a coffee sack: over 600,000.
- Number of baskets of coffee beans (called cherries, pictured at right) plantation workers can pick per day: 10.
- Number of cups of coffee 10 baskets of cherries can produce: 2,400.
- Number of harvested beans considered premium quality: 20%.
- All coffee plantations are located between the Tropic of Cancer to the north and Tropic of Capricorn to the south.
- The arabica, still growing wild in Ethiopia, is the original coffee plant.
- Number of Arabica coffee cherries to make up one pound of roasted coffee: 2,000.

➪ Number of beans in one cherry: 2.

➪ Number of years a coffee tree produces beans: 15 to 20.

➪ Coffee trees self-pollinate. Coffee ripens on the same branch differently, displaying ripe red berries, unripe green berries, and overripe black berries: pickers pluck the reds.

➪ Like grapes, coffee bean production relies on the appropriate altitude, soil conditions, rainfall, drainage, and temperature.

➪ Number of countries that grow coffee commercially: 45.

➪ The country that provides one-third of the world's coffee: Brazil.

➪ Number of pounds Brazil produces per year: 3.3 billion pounds.

➪ Number of Brazilians employed in Brazil's coffee industry: 5 million.

➪ Lyrics from "The Coffee Song" sung by Frank Sinatra: "They add coffee to the coffee in Brazil" and "they gotta gang of coffee in Brazil."

➪ Caffeine content directly relates to altitude: the less caffeine content the higher the beans are grown.

➪ Number of pounds of coffee cherries one acre of coffee trees produces: 10,000.

➪ Number of times coffee is bought and sold before you get a cup: 6.

➪ Coffee fiend J. S. Bach about his

favourite stimulant: "the most precious of blisses."

- J. S. Bach composed a coffee cantata in 1732.
- Number of beans Beethoven counted out for each cup of coffee he brewed: 60.
- French philosopher Voltaire, it was reported, drained 50 cups of coffee a day to come up with pithy quips such as: "Judge a man by his questions rather than his answers."

Withdrawal symptoms:

- pounding headaches, fatigue, vertigo, nausea.

Drawbacks from downing two to four (eight-ounce) cups of coffee daily:

1) diminishing bone density (osteoporosis risk)
2) conception troubles
3) premature births
4) low birth weights
5) health risk for those with gout or high blood pressure
6) Remarkably, "At a given time, the human body will absorb 300 milligrams of caffeine, additional caffeine is cast off, 20% dissipated each hour."

- From another scientific study: "Steam rising from a cup of coffee contains the same amount of antioxidants as do 3 oranges: antioxidants being heterocyclic compounds that work to prevent cancers

> ▶ Number of cups drank over four hours to be lethal: 100

and heart diseases." (Inhale deeply, friends, it's good for you.)

- ⇨ Uh-oh: on the International Olympic Committee list of prohibited substances—caffeine.
- ⇨ Hey, you deep-frowners on the Olympic Committee: coffee was originally employed by some monastic orders as an aid to prayer (not unknown at sporting events).
- ⇨ This from a Nova Scotia sailing ship's log: "Coffee is much preferable to tea, the water being so bad."
- ⇨ Number of weeks for roasted beans to shed some flavour: 2.
- ⇨ Number of hours for ground coffee to lose peak flavour: 1.
- ⇨ Time for brewed coffee or espresso to flatten in taste: within minutes.
- ⇨ Blends make up the majority the majority of coffee consumed.

The most expensive (fifty dollars U.S. per cup) and rarest coffee in the world—maybe in the entire Milky Way—comes from Sumatra, where coffee plantation workers collect the fecal droppings of the Asian Palm Civet. The droppings are laden with ripe, indigestible coffee beans fermented by the animal's stomach acid and enzymation action. Word of warning: This brew doesn't come readily on-demand here as a double-double. Not that you would wish it.

The best coffee anywhere?

In the opinion of coffee experts? Jamaican Blue Mountain. Except some coffee sybarites insist that the pure Jamaican Blue Mountain found on the island of St. Helena's (off North West Africa) is superior. No double-doubles here either.

Of course the majority of Nova Scotians frequent chains for their caffeine hits, favouring, in the main, the heavyweight, Tim Horton's. Statistically, Tim Horton's (a.k.a. Canadian crack) claims sixty-two percent of the Canadian coffee market, with Starbucks in the number two position, nabbing seven percent. There are tea nations, and there are coffee nations. Canada, hey, we're a Timbit nation.

The get-up-and-go-get-'em guy behind the Tim Horton's "hot coffee and a donut to go" powerhouse is Ron Joyce of Tatamagouche, Nova Scotia. A former Hamilton, Ontario, cop, Joyce partnered up with hockey star Tim Horton in 1964 to create their institutional success story. Unfortunately for Tim Horton, it was short-lived. With the pair boasting forty outlets in 1974, all-star Sabre defenceman Horton, driving home to Toronto from Buffalo, New York, after an NHL game, lost control of his sports car and died. (Later, many eyebrows rose when, mindful of Horton's grisly demise, Timbits—an unwitting but nevertheless dubious name choice—made an appearance as a store staple.) Joyce bought out Horton's widow's business interest and aggressively expanded the chain to icon status. The chain now has close to three thousand outlets nationwide. The ratio Joyce uses: one Tim Horton's to every fifteen thousand people. (Nova Scotia must be defying that corporate ratio, for it seems there's a Tim Horton's on every corner you pass.)

"R-r-r-roll up the rim to win," "Timmy's," and "double-double" shouldered their way into the Canadian lexicon. Over the years, an urban legend began that Tim Horton's coffee's impact derived from jolts of nicotine staff added to the brew. On February 3, 2004, a Tim's coffee sample analyzed by laboratory chromatography (a flame ionization process) debunked the nicotine story (the test found no trace of MSG either).

In 1995, Tim Horton's and the American fast food giant Wendy's merged. Joyce continued to lead Timbit Nation until finally easing back to concentrate on charitable works, such as summer camps for economically disadvantaged kids (the first camp was established in Malagash, Nova Scotia). Either as an underage bar for teens and older students (who sometimes suffer from caffeine overdoses), or as a centre for a social life with donuts, most Nova Scotians will say unequivocally that "they've always got time for Tim Horton's."

Preparing coffee from *Kitchen Directory and American Housewife* (1844):

> "Use a tablespoon of ground to a pint of boiling water. Boil in a tin pot for 20 to 25 minutes. If boiled longer, it will not taste fresh and lively. Let stand 4 to 5 minutes to settle. Pour off grounds into a coffee pot or urn. Put fish skin or isinglass size of a nine-pence in the pot when put on to boil or else the white and shell of half an egg to a couple of quarts of coffee."

Excerpted from a 2007 Nova Scotia personal injury lawyer law blog:

- ⇨ McDonald's requires its restaurant franchises to serve coffee at 80 to 88 degrees Celsius—a burn hazard.
- ⇨ Coffee held in a pot must be kept at 85°C—definitely a burn hazard.
- ⇨ McDonald's assumes customers realize their coffee comes to them piping hot.
- ⇨ Between 1982 and 1992, McDonald's received more than seven hundred burn complaints, including to children and infants, which resulted in more than a few large damage payouts and scald-faker dismissals.

From a CBC news item

"A Nova Scotia man who was arrested after riding his horse through a coffee shop drive-through will stand trial after withdrawing his guilty plea." (A double-double of hay for the vehicle, sir?)

THE LANGUAGE OF ESPRESSO TO BE SPOKEN HERE IN NOVA SCOTIA

Espresso, many discerning Nova Scotian coffee aficionados will tell you, is the "pinnacle of coffee drinking." In Italy, coffee and espresso are one in the same, and such an essential of Italian daily life that the government regulates its price. Espresso first showed up in Italy in the late ninteenth century and then disconcertingly disappeared, only to reappear in 1946 when Gaggia, an Italian manufacturing company, invented a device to make the beverage. A typical espresso is freshly ground coffee immediately brewed: a two -ounce "shot" of caffeine plus added foam. A caffe latte is an espresso shot mixed with hot steamed milk. Many in Nova Scotia ask for either a latte or a double latte. And of course, the server complies with their requests. But ask for a latte in Italy and what'll you get? A glass of milk. It's all in the language spoken.

▶ Did you know that coffee shares with beer and peanut butter the distinction of being one of the ten most recognizable odours?

▶ Did you know that the British favour instant coffee 10 to 1 over freshly brewed? Keeps their upper lips stiff.

▶ How about that "for reducing wrinkles and improving skin, the Japanese have known to bathe in coffee grounds fermented with pineapple pulp"?

You say you like a good cappuccino? For those of you who have yet to enjoy this beverage, here's the recipe for it. One-third espresso, one-third hot steamed milk, and the last third, foamed milk. You can add sugar to taste. The Italians named the drink cappuccino ("cap") because they laughingly thought espresso coffee mixed with or topped with steamed milk bore a striking similarity to the dark to mid-brown tone of a Capuchin friar's habit and the milky "cap" of the monk's tonsured noggin.

Maybe you don't like your coffee strong. So you opt for decaf. You're not alone.

➪ Twelve percent of total worldwide java consumption, or a billion pounds per year, is decaf. The process of decaffeinating coffee first emerged from the lab of German scientist Ludwig Roselius in 1905. He used a sketchy, potentially poisonous hydrocarbon called benzene "to remove caffeine from premoistened green coffee beans." These days, decaffeinating firms take three paths to the same end.

➪ The first is favoured by health food stores—that would be the Swiss water process. Beans are simply soaked in water, and the caffeine's extracted. Decaffeinated water is then "reunited with the caffeine-less beans." But it's argued that more flavour is lost this way than with the others.

➪ The second methodology uses methyl chloride, and follows the Swiss water process closely, veering off form when methyl chloride is "added to extracted water to bond with caffeine molecules." This "new compound is removed from the water," thereby leaving more of the flavour intact. For those of you wild-eyed and clutching at your throats at the mention of methyl chloride, chill out. The U.S. Food and Drug Administration says that less than trace amounts of methyl chloride can be found in the decaf product. So no health hazard.

➪ The third method eschews methyl chloride for a "naturally occurring" solvent chemical extracted from decaying organic material (such as sugar cane, bananas, and apples) called ethyl acetate, which bonds with caffeine molecules. To be classified as decaf, coffee must be ninety-eight percent caffeine-free. Oh, about that leftover caffeine? It's sold to pharmaceutical companies. Warning for decaf drinkers: robusta coffee packs more than twice as much caffeine wallop as arabica.

Coffee, as it turns out, accepts other flavours openly. Store shelves bulge with astonishing coffee combos. In case you're wondering how your cup of Orange Vienna got to be Orange Vienna, your flavoured coffee is produced like this: After roasting, the beans are cooled to 100°C. Pores opened, the beans are "more receptive to applied flavours." Most popular tastes? Irish cream and hazelnut with fruit or citrus-based flavours are among the top ten favourites. Nothing truly contemporary in this. The first coffee drinkers, Arabs, enhanced their brewing coffee with spices. In the 1600s, Europeans candied-up their coffee with chocolate. Germany's Frederick the Great doctored his brews with champagne and a tat of mustard.

Coffee fared well as a stimulant to business and for business. The famous British insurance giant Lloyd's of London began its days as Edward Lloyd's Coffeehouse. Coffee houses showed up in Nova Scotia's past, too. From a Thomas Raddall account of Nova Scotian life from 1775 to 1783:

> "Country folk up for the market frequented the Crown Coffee House in Upper Water Street near the dockyard. Every St Patrick's Day, a group of Irishmen dined together at Sutherland's Coffee House in Bedford Row. Freemasons met sometimes at the Golden Ball but more often at the Wolf Inn on Granville Street, opposite Government House.
>
> 1788 Merchants of Granville Street build a broad wooden walk from Buckingham Street to the corner of George, down George to Hollis. Became the 'Change (Exchange) of Halifax, where merchants, ship owners and

financiers gathered every fine morning from 11 to 12 to discuss their affairs. In cold or wet weather, they held their meetings over coffee in the Guild of Merchants' chamber of the Pontac Inn, a sort of transatlantic Lloyd's."

So where did this coffee beverage (only exceeded by tea and water as the most popular drink worldwide) come from?

⇨ The coffee tree itself is an evergreen that grows to, tops, fifteen feet in height. Most coffee trees throughout the forty-five countries currently producing coffee cherries are pruned back to eight feet, which makes life somewhat less of a reach for pickers.

Before the cherries appear, small, highly aromatic, short-lived flowers blossom, which then evolve into cranberry-sized coffee cherries. A coffee tree matures in four to five years and yields crops for between twelve and fifteen years. Like wine and beer, coffee originates in the Middle East. Ancient Abyssinia (today's Ethiopia)—where the original coffee plant, the arabica, continues to grow wild—is the source region. A story taken with less of a grain of salt than others circulating about the discovery of coffee rolls like this. About AD 800 to 850, a goat herder named Kaldi saw some of his goats leaping and gamboling about with a frisky abandon seldom seen under a blazing, energy-sapping sun. Puzzled and curious, Kaldi payed closer scrutiny to his charges' grazing choices. The animals excitedly bounding to and fro, he observed, did so after chowing down on a particular shrub's leaves and berries. In the spirit of nothing ventured, nothing gained, Kaldi popped some coffee beans into his mouth. And tentatively chewed, faster and faster. He abruptly felt more alert than an antelope in a pride of lions. It was not known if he then took the first unofficial coffee break to draw conclusions from his experiment with the plant's beans. But when he stopped gamboling himself, he determined what made his goats so hyper.

Of Kaldi and his subsequent status after discovering coffee, scholarship and myth-making is scant. We may not know Kaldi. But we know coffee. And we take much comfort in that. Arabs initially used it as a stimulant (naturally), as a medicine, and as a wine. Interestingly, coffee was first known in Europe as Arabian wine. In the fourteenth century, Arabs, the first to brew coffee, cultivated coffee trees commercially in the Arabian Peninsula in close proximity to the port of Mocha. Coffee assumed such a status in Arab family life that "one of the causes allowed by law for marital separation is the husband's refusal to brew up pots of coffee for his wife." Sounds reasonable. Nomadic tribes, for long caravans, took to preserving coffee cherries. In the 1400s, an edict from the Qu'ran forbade consuming alcohol. So devotees of Islam switched to coffee. Coffee-poetry emerged in Mecca when four verses on the beverage were penned in 1511. Thirteenth-century Turks roasted and ground coffee beans and three hundred years later in the 1500s, Turkey flexed its commercial muscle as the chief distributor of coffee, supplying markets developed in Egypt, Syria, Persia (Iran), and Venice, Italy. Two coffee houses opened for business in Constantinople and in 1554, reported boffo business. Many more followed. By 1600, coffee was huge throughout the Oriental world—and elsewhere. In 1683, the price per pound of coffee in New York was $4.98.

Coffee as a medicine hit its highest and lowest levels of English popularity in the 1600s

➪ More and more invasively bizarre medical contraptions were employed to administer mixtures of coffee, heated butter, honey, and oil curatives. In self-defence, Brits, faced with the enema within, bypassed coffee and instituted tea as the British Isle's national beverage. For English diehards clinging to the non-medicinal usage (and enjoyment) of coffee, the Swiss firm

Nestlé bettered British coffee-drinking lives when the company invented instant coffee in 1937. The "quick-coffee" granules Nestlé had been on the quest for as far back as 1867, were called Nescafé, and the Brits, who preferred instant to fresh brewed, called it perfection.

Coffee time today means leaving a lighter coffee stain on the environment and thinking outside the cup and beyond the mug. For instance, some coffee chains now utilize biodegradable coffee containers. Enlightened coffee drinkers do their java bit to save the planet by filling their coffee needs with fair trade products certified as processed under socially and environmentally fair conditions. As you socialize over cups of coffee with friends, old and new, think on what famous French novelist Honoré de Balzac once quipped: "When we drink coffee, ideas march in like the army."

SODA AND WATER

SODA POPS

In 1828, German Jacob Schweppe mucked about with a liquid blending of quinine (used first by the Indian Army to combat malaria) and sugar and came up with an Indian tonic water.

- ➪ Schweppe went on to found the British soft drink firm that still bears his name and sells his tonic water (a great friend of gin).
- ➪ We go now to 1895: John Pemberton, an American chemist from Atlanta, Georgia, messed around with a nut extract, sugar, caffeine, coco leaves, vegetable extracts, and soda water, and came up with a world-beater soft drink called Coca-Cola.
- ➪ Coca-Cola's distinctive bottle took its shape from the cola nut.
- ➪ In Nova Scotia's pioneer days, a non-alcoholic drink came from boiling spruce tree tips.

A contemporary description from a blog on the taste of non-alcoholic spruce beer:

> "This is the worst. It's overwhelmingly tree sap and not the nice bits of trees like birch beer, root beer, sarsaparilla. You know they make hot dogs out of all the parts you can't use anywhere else. This must be soda's equivalent to a hot dog. The flavour is pine and menthol."

- ➪ Root beer: a sweetened carbonated drink made from the root of a sassafras plant or the bark of a sassafras tree blended with sarsaparilla spice.
- ➪ Birch beer: akin to root beer except it's flavoured with the bark of birch trees.

MAYBE NOT COKE OR PEPSI, BUT OURS

Metegan River. 1921. A place back then with a significant drawback for any outside-the-box machine-assisted enterprise: namely, no electrical power. Faced with that wrinkle, it behooves you, therefore, to figure that establishing a soda pop company would rank right up there with, say, manufacturing extension cords for the neighbours. But since when did drawbacks ever flummox hot-to-trot entrepreneurs with a vision? Count among those indefatigable go-getters the team of Edward Belliveau, his son Emile, and his pal Johnny Boudreau—establishers of Clare's Original Pop. Belt-driving motors ran some of the operations. What was in the pop plant? Two tubs for bottle washing, a bottling machine, a large pop-preparation tank, and a modest-sized stove for heating.

Pop production burbled along from Monday to Thursday. Orange, strawberry, sarsaparilla, root beer, lime, cream soda, raspberry, cherry, and ginger ale (golden and dry). A cola came later.

Overnight, sugar was dissolved in the preparation tank. Next morning, the popsters added citric acid, flavour, and colour to the sweetened solution. Two taste sensations were made each production day. Then on Friday and Saturday, the Clare's Original Pop truck delivered the week's output to retail sites between Beaver River and Smith's Cove. Digby Neck received its throat quenchers via ferry. Price per case of twenty-four: eighty-five cents. With no refrigeration, the Belliveaus and Boudreau used a "natchul" solution to the cooling problem. They kept their pop "on ice"—blocks of it, cut in the winter months from nearby lakes and "stored under sawdust for summer use" in a building for just that usage. Local retailers selling Clare's Original Pop relied on "ice boxes" (insulated storage units chilled by ice). Hard times hit the popsters during the Second World War years. Sugar rationing shut them down. Later, and happily, the company rebounded. Now under the proprietorship of Gilles Comeau, Clare's Original Pop continues to serve up orange, cream soda, lime, root beer, strawberry, and ginger ale beverages manufactured in the traditional manner to maintain Clare's Original taste. Only the equipment has changed.

SCOTLAND'S OTHER NATIONAL DRINK (AND A CAPE BRETON VERSION)

Irn-Bru, lauded in Scotland as "the grrrreat curative for a hangover" brought on by unrestrained benders of that other national drink, whisky, does only what every other carbonated, sugar-loaded drink does for heavy drinkers: replace lost liquids and depleted body sugars. Made from a tightly guarded formula (a written copy is stashed in a Swiss bank vault), the unnaturally vibrant orange soft drink, chemists say, bears traces of ammonium ferric citrate (for that slight citrus flavour), sugars, caffeine (Red Bull, V, and Red Devil mimic Irn-Bru's jolting "restorative" effect), quinine, and colouring (E 110 and E 124). A now-defunct (ceasing operations in 1990) Cape Breton concern by the name of McKinley-Mckinlay Soft Drink Company put on offer a non-licensed beverage they called Iron Brew. Iron Brew nixed caffeine. And quinine. In fact, the drink eschewed just about everything else that could link it to Scotland's Irn-Bru. Take colour. Unlike Irn-Bru's florescent orange that no one sober could find anywhere in the natural world, Iron Brew existed as a brown, fruity-tasting cola, reminiscent of Dr. Pepper and Fanta. Pepsi-Cola took the beverage over, marketing the drink, now monikered Cape Breton's Irn-Bru, in plain plastic bottles with simple black lettering on a white label—complete with a disclaimer that Cape Breton's Irn-Bru was not a source of iron. Not a source of longevity either. Cape Breton's Irn-Bru disappeared, defunct like the McKinley-Mckinlay Soft Drink Company.

"POP-ELLER" TAKES OFF

The Propeller Brewing Company manufactures four "unique delicious all-natural sodas." The firm's root beer, ginger beer, orange soda, and vanilla cream soda come caffeine-free and without preservatives (like their beers). These old-style sodas are splendid to quaff. The ginger beer (with ginseng added for an energy booster), the company insists, is "great also as mix for popular cocktails such as the Dark and Stormy and the Moscow Mule." Propeller root beer (using cane sugar for sweetener) poured over vanilla ice cream in a large glass makes a super float.

Propeller cream soda, brewed in small batches unlike commercial Chemical City cream sodas, uses natural flavours and sweetens up with Annapolis Valley honey, contributing to a "smooth, creamy flavour." Lastly, the Euro-style orange soda. These are definitely not soft drink beverages to "fly under the radar." Prepare for taste lift-off, friends.

FRESH WATER: THE BEVERAGE THAT TRULY REFRESHES

We take potable water for granted. Water's always been there for us and, we casually assume, here for us to exploit forever and ever. As listed by the World Business Council for Sustainable Development, water is "food, energy, transportation, nature, leisure, identity, culture, social norms and virtually all the products used on a daily basis." For decades, Nova Scotians have relied on streams, coastal ocean currents, and tides to "dilute and assimilate wastes." Only recently have we been feeling flushed with embarrassment with our longtime indifference at the consequences of our actions.

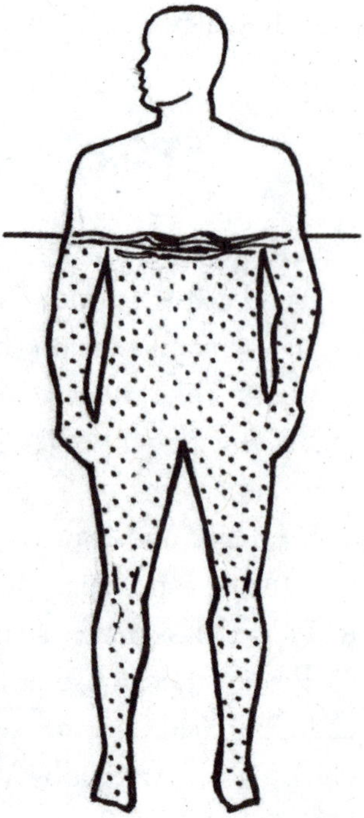

We know it to be a given that water is essential to life. The evidence? Of all beverages drank worldwide, water is number one, well ahead of the number two and three beverages: coffee and tea. Our bodies are seventy percent water. We need regular rehydration to keep our systems working tip-top. A normal, well-nourished person, studies note, has a capability of surviving up to eight weeks without an intake of food. Without water, however, life peters out after no more than a few days. Without water in our system, digestion, transportation of basic nutrients and their vital absorption and bodily wastes disposal, and internal temperature regulation collapses. It's therefore no wonder that Pindar, the great nine-lyric poet of ancient Greece, named two parts hydrogen and one part oxygen "the noblest of the elements." Others have had their say, too. Some wise, prescient, cautionary, and droll observations, axioms, and quips of note worth considering:

- ➪ From the venerable Chinese philosopher and thinker Lao-Tsze (654 BC–531 BC): "Nothing on earth is so weak and yielding as water, but for breaking down the firm and strong, it has no equal."
- ➪ Poet W. H. Auden: "Thousands have lived without love, not one without water."
- ➪ From Paolo Lugari, the founder of the Gaviotas Community in Colombia: "Civilization has been a permanent dialogue between human beings and water."
- ➪ From Albert Szent-Gyorgyi, Hungarian biochemist and Nobel Prize winner for medicine: "Water is life's matter and matrix, mother and medium. There is no life without water."
- ➪ Comment by Rachel Carson, author of *Silent Spring*: "In an age when man has forgotten his origins and is blind even to his most essential needs for survival, water along with other resources has become the victim of his indifference."
- ➪ Benjamin Franklin (1706–1790), American brainiac, polymath, and overachiever: "When the well is dry, we learn the worth of water."
- ➪ From the Qu'ran 21:30: "By means of water, we give life in everything."

- Professor Emeritus, University of California, Dr. Helen Ingram: "Almost everywhere, water is underpriced."
- An American Indian saying: "The frog does not drink up the pond in which he lives."
- The wonderful curmudgeon, humourist, and novelist Mark Twain in 1884: "Whisky is for drinking; water is for fighting over."
- From the late American stand-up comedian and irrepressible boozer, Joe E. Lewis: "Water's just whisky with all the beneficial ingredients removed. Or, 100-proof humidity."
- A definition of water from *The Devil's Dictionary* by Ambrose Bierce: "Water's a medicine for the cure of thirst."

WATER WATER EVERYWHERE: WHERE WE GET OUR DROPS TO DRINK

Nova Scotia's lakes, rivers, and aquifer system (groundwater) watersheds are drawn upon, sometimes heavily, to supply provincial water needs. Artesian wells and mechanically pumped deep wells collect groundwater for the use of numerous rural and outlying town or city households. This water treks through metres of soils and rock strata, which behave as natural filters to render the water microbiologically safe for consumption. Unfortunately, the safety system the aquifer provides can be breached. Wells require timely intervention if leachates from contaminant sources such as industrial, agricultural, or landfill sites compromise water wholesomeness, and necessitate treatment if unsafe levels of calcium

ions, arsenic, iron, manganese, or other chemicals have been detected by water sample trials. The thinking from water quality experts on the purity of provincial lakes and rivers is that, generally, those bodies contain organic and fecal components "washed" into them from various bordering land surfaces.

SETTING CRITERIA FOR SAFE DRINKING WATER STANDARDS

▶ *Guidelines for Canadian Drinking Water* counsels and recommends reasonable levels for pH content, colour, total coliform organizations, fluoride, iron, arsenic, copper, pesticides, dissolved solids, and cesium.

- ⇨ Cited blame for microbiological contamination: farming, logging, and wildlife pee and poop.
- ⇨ Microbial contaminants: viruses and bacteria.
- ⇨ Inorganic contaminants: salts and metals.
- ⇨ Organic contaminants: pesticides, herbicides, organic chemical by-products of industrial processes, storm water runoffs, leachates from faulty septic systems and gas stations.
- ⇨ Radioactive contaminants: naturally occurring materials or those traceable back to oil, gas, and mining activities.
- ⇨ Turbidity (cloudiness) sources: minute soil particles and acidity and discolouration from decomposing vegetative matter.

Watersheds overseen by the Halifax Regional Water Commission:

- ⇨ Pockwock Lake: supplies water for Halifax, Bedford, Sackville, Timberlea, Fall River, and Waverley.

- ➪ Tomahawk Lake: designated future water supply.
- ➪ Chain Lake: Halifax's backup supply source.
- ➪ Lamont/Topsail: Dartmouth's backup water supply.
- ➪ Lake Major: supplies water for Dartmouth, Cole Harbour, Westphal, Eastern Passage, North Preston, Cherrybrook, and Montague Gold Mines.

Other provincial watersheds:

- ➪ Lake George, serving Yarmouth;
- ➪ lakes of the Mersey watershed, feeding Annapolis Royal and Digby's water systems; and
- ➪ the tar-pond troubled Muggah Creek watershed near Sydney.

SOBERING WATER WORRIES

Issues

- ➪ Housing developers routinely and relentlessly infill wetlands, thereby devastating wildlife habitat and natural soil erosion protectorates with seeming impunity.
- ➪ Halifax regional lakes are "dying rapidly because of

> ▶ Watershed protection: the Nova Scotia Environment Act imposes restrictions on fishing, hunting, and the use of motorized vehicles near these areas.

high concentrations of phosphorus, nitrogen, other nutrients from fertilizer run-off, households, agriculture and forestry."

What a lake's water quality depends on, in expert environmentalists' opinions:

- ⇨ a robust watershed, coniferous and deciduous forests of all ages, not altogether susceptible to the ravages of disease or insect infestation;
- ⇨ enlightened leadership to devise savvy conservation policies and measures for better stewardship of soil, wildlife, and water to prevent further water resource losses and their spin-off, economic deterioration;
- ⇨ "increased emphasis on water recycling"; and
- ⇨ "increased public awareness of the growing costs of obtaining high-quality water."

WATER TREATMENT: "A SERIES OF PROCESSES APPLIED IN SEQUENCE"

Four measures to "address microbiological, chemical and aesthetic issues": containment, capture, treatment, and dispersion.

The most effective water treatment systems

- ⇨ Sedimentation: alum and iron salts, or synthetic organic polymers, form tiny, sticky particles called "floc" that draw dirt particles to them, which, combined, sink as sediment to the tank's base.
- ⇨ Filtration: makes use of sand, gravel, and charcoal filters to eradicate all bothersome tinier particulates from the water, such as

SODA & WATER

clays, silts, and natural organic matter, which clarifies the water and enhances the effectiveness of the disinfection stage.

⇨ Ion exchange: if sedimentation and filtration comes up a bit short, this treatment process can rid hard water of inorganic contaminants, arsenic, chromium, excess fluoride, nitrates, radium, and uranium.

⇨ Adsorption: organic contaminants and undesirable colour-, taste-, and odour-causing compounds love to adhere to granula or powdered, glue-like activated carbon surfaces, which makes them easier to dispose of.

⇨ Disinfection: effective employment of chlorine, chloramines, or chlorine dioxide, together with powerful disinfectant ozone and ultraviolet radiation, whacks unto death nasty and dangerous microbes. Chlorine deals well with disquieting colour and taste removal, controlling odour, and clamping down on algal growth. Even though carcinogenic trihalomethanes can be caused by water chlorification, the risk factor, as explained by scientists, is minimal: "if one million people drank water for a period of 70 years with the amount of chemical in it equal to the standard, 1 person would probably get cancer from the drinking water."

⇨ Dispersal: top-quality drinking water flows through pipes to homes and businesses.

Comments from Sara Wilson, a Nova Scotia ecologist:

"Despite an overall increase in quality, more than a third of Nova Scotians don't trust their water. About 18% of households purchase bottled water for an estimated $265 per year and 16% use water filters."

WATER FLOWS UPHILL TOWARDS MONEY

They blitz us in print, TV, and radio ads. In stores. On T-shirts. Bottled water jive. You've seen "the product" on grocery and convenience store shelves: row upon row of rippled plastic bottles brandishing labels depicting crystalline pure water cascading from airy mountain springs. Or pristine freshwater lakes with airbrushed sparkles. The lengths bottled water companies go to for quenching our thirsts. Or do they? Are we being fooled? Often we are.

Despite the alluring packaging, the majority of bottled water comes from the same source as the water from your tap. According to Ideal Bite, an online source for green and healthy living, up to forty percent of bottled water originates from municipal water supplies. Pepsi-Cola, bottlers and purveyors of Aquafina, have admitted as much. Spell Evian backwards, friends, and you'll get what bottled water drinkers with ready safe municipal water availability at hand must be: naive. Bottled water, as mounting and damning evidence attests to, is proving to be very costly to the consumer's wallet and to the environment—a definitive hazard to the health of both.

THE HOW-SO'S

- Scratched or heat-exposed plastic bottles leach chemicals linked to cancer and birth defects, such as phthalates and bisphenol-A into the water.
- The shipping of bottled water worldwide results in an ecologically damaging carbon footprint.
- Number of years for tossed away or landfilled plastic bottles to biodegrade: 1,000.

WHAT TO DO?

With bottled water sales at all-time highs, turning massive profits for corporations such as Dasani's parent, Coca-Cola, and Aquafina's Pepsi-Cola, consumers could switch back to municipal water streamed through faucet or pitcher filters. Add a drop or two of lemon or lime juice to your glass or pitcher if you crave a pleasing flavour. Carry a thermos of chilled tap water on your rounds.

A REVELATORY EXPERIMENT

In 2006, the Halifax Regional Water Commission made an arresting discovery. They bottled HRWC tap water from Pockwock Lake in fifty thousand units and advertised it as "H 2 O: Tap Into Great Water." All fifty thousand units went. Fast. Like water down a wide drain. A lesson here, folks?

STILL AT POCKWOCK LAKE

The J. Douglas Kline Water Treatment Plant, in conjunction with the Natural Science and Engineering Council and Dalhousie University, will "adopt water quality master planning to create a centre for water quality excellence in North America." Refreshing.

The last word on water goes to the sagacious wit, novelist, and wise man Samuel Langhorne Clemens (1835–1910), better known as Mark Twain:

"Water,
taken in moderation,
cannot hurt anybody."

LAST CALL

The first European explorers and colonists found Nova Scotia a bountiful source of natural resources ripe for exploitation. They also found harsh seasonal conditions, loneliness, despair, and the very real possibility that their lives had the potential of being nasty, brutish, and short. Existence fell to tough slogs of logging, fishing, and trapping. Evenings for the literate meant huddling for warmth by a fire, scrawling down singular accounts and impressions of the New World for the good folks back home. (In the dead of winter, ink froze. Just one more lousy thing to numb them clear through to the bone.) Illiterates, on the other hand, relied on cheap rum for their stimulation and entertainment needs. Condemned to wait for spring when their ink would thaw, the literates too found solace in the ardent spirit. And so began the beverage shaping of community life in Nova Scotia by non-indigenous peoples. Over the passing years, widening circles of rum's influence rippled through the temples of commerce and the halls of governance in times often bullish with entrepreneurial zeal and fractious dust-ups between competing French and British nationals. These contretemps included sanctioned looting, rampaging, and of course, that old standby, pillaging. Who in the hard-scrabble 1700s, or deep in the contentious years of rum, religion, and the temperance movement backlash, would have ever imagined or foreseen the province transformed into a land mass pregnant with the promise to supercede thc traditional wine country climes of Southern France, Spain, Italy, South Africa, Australia, and Southern California? Far from being over and done with, beverage's power to mould Nova Scotian life continues, undoubtedly with many more twists and turns to come.

ACKNOWLEDGEMENTS

I am grateful for the invaluable scholarship and information plucked from: *The Tangled Vine: Winegrowing in Nova Scotia* by Chris Naugler, Bruce Wright, and Robert Murray; *What's Brewing: Oland 1867–1971: A History* by G. Brenton Haliburton; *When Rum Was King* by Barry Grant; *Tempered By Rum* by James Morrison and James Moreira; *On Both Sides of the Law* by Hugh H. Corkum; *The Life and Times of Alexander Keith* by Peter MacCreath; *Halifax, Warden of the North* by Thomas Raddall; *The Dark Side of Life in Victorian Halifax* by Judith Fingard; and *Tea Tips*, a booklet published by J. E. Morse Teas. Other information sources (and there were many) are generally acknowledged throughout the text. Lastly, I am most grateful to Sandra McIntyre for the opportunity to plunge into the drink.